MW01065267

Praise for *Is Your Child A Money Master or a Money Monster?*

"Your child's future starts the day they are born. Help them see the importance of living a life full of value, education, and ambition. Do not put Sunny's book down!"

—*Erica L. McCain, LUTCF*
Member MDRT, and author of Ladies With Loot

"A critical issue we face in America is the training for our children to fully develop to become responsible, dependable and happy. Happiness is a byproduct of how we operate and who we are. I certainly will share this book with my children so they can help their children because I believe it will help the whole person in addition to helping him become financially secure. I know that many people will not make the effort it will take to teach these truths to their children, but those who do will be richly rewarded."

—*William H. Cain*
Chief Executive Officer, Financial Independence Group

IS YOUR CHILD A MONEY **MASTER** OR A MONEY **MONSTER?**

IS YOUR CHILD A MONEY **MASTER** OR A MONEY **MONSTER?**

Seven Habits of Highly Motivated Kids for Financial Success

SUNNY LEE

Investment Advisor Representative (IAR®)

First edition

For more information, contact:
Twin Sprouts Publishing
www.nomoneymonster.com

Printed in the United States of America

Library of Congress Control Number: 2015918481

ISBN Paperback: 978-0-692-50854-1
ISBN eBook: 978-0-692-50855-8

Cover design: Michelle Manley
Interior design: Ghislain Viau

First of all, thank you Father God and Lord Jesus for helping me to finish this book.

Next, my humble effort I dedicate to my awesome twin boys Jason & Matthew. My sons, this is my gift for you and I love you more than you can ever imagine.

Along with my good neighbors Mr. Vince & Ms. Kelly who encouraged me and inspired me to consider publishing this book.

Finally, thank you Appa!

"The present is a constant drip of future reality."
—Sunny Lee (mommy, now)

"When you love me, I am perfect.
When I love you, you are perfect.
Love is what makes everything perfect."
—Jason J Lee (son, at age four)

About this Book

Sunny Lee is an Investment Advisor Representative in Southern California and proud mother of twin boys. She wants them to be Money Masters, not Money Monsters!

From the time they were only two years old, she began teaching them about money management. To do that, she developed a reward system for the efforts they successfully completed with a good attitude. As they grew, so did her expectations of them. Now, at only eleven years old, they have savings accounts, investment accounts, and college funds — all of which the boys fund themselves and manage with the help of their mom.

Sunny's creative system took the struggle out of getting ready for school, taught her boys about taxes, saving for college, sharing with others, and improved their writing skills!

By following the method in this book, your child can become a Money Master, too!

Contents

Introduction

Children are much smarter than we think. They are like sponges, soaking up knowledge and behaviors from watching those around them. As parents, we are their first source of both. We teach them about nature and how to be safe. We show them how to ride a bicycle, and manage social relationships, so that they can become their best selves. We help them develop social skills. We do this because we want them to be masters in their lives, not monsters in society.

But how many of us actively show our children how to manage their money? My parents taught me many things, but managing money wasn't one of them.

Money is essential to a safe, comfortable life, but many of us aren't taught how to make, handle, or save it. What's more, because of this lack of skill, many people don't have adequate financial resources to allow them the pleasure of being able to give to others.

Putting money in its place and using it to make a good life is something your children can learn easily. And they can learn it at a very young age, long before they need to apply for scholarships or buy their first cars.

I am a financial advisor. Every day, I work with people to help them invest and save wisely. Many of my clients have enough money, and others don't. Everyone who comes to me learns what it means to be a master of their own finances, instead of a slave to every single dollar. Sometimes, this learning requires a big shift in their attitude and spending habits; it often requires them to learn new skills.

I am also the happy mother of twin boys, Jason and Matthew. From the beginning, it was important to me that my sons understood financial security. When they were only two years old, I began showing them the value of money—how one gets it, and what to do with it.

If we aren't the masters of our money, we are helpless slaves to it. Money can become a monster in our lives if we don't learn to control, manage, and save it. It leaks out here and there in unconscious spending until it's gone and we have nothing to show for it. Even worse, we constantly need to bow to others' demands for payment. We scramble to pay bills and end up living to work instead of enjoying our lives and working to live.

But that unhappy scenario is something we can teach our children to avoid. Regardless of age, gender, or social status, we are in charge of our finances. Teaching our children to have mastery over their money is critical to their future success. We want them to be Money Masters, not Money Monsters.

Learning money mastery can be fun for children and parents alike! In fact, learning *should* be fun, especially for young children. Because I taught my boys about money principles, it made life easier for our entire family. Even better, they learned to *love* their own success!

But how do we teach our children about money?

In this book, I will show you the seven simple habits I taught my sons in order to make them Money Masters. Instead of depending on me to give money to them and tell them what to do, they have learned how to make, save, give, and use their own money.

Have you ever heard the expression, "Give a man a fish and he will eat for a day; teach a man to fish and he will eat for a lifetime"? Learning how to manage your money—to make it do what you want—is like being the man who learns to catch his own fish so he can eat whenever he wants. Teaching your children to control their money guarantees not only that they will eat for their lifetimes, but also that they will thrive throughout their lives.

However, the drive to acquire money at any cost—but with as little effort as possible—can create Money Monsters who will do anything to get more cash … even extreme, heartless things. People with this mindset will beg, borrow, or steal. They may kill, terrorize, or defraud others in order to put money in their pockets without putting in the effort to earn it legitimately. The development of a healthy mental approach to money begins at the beginning, when our children are very young.

Money can't buy happiness, as the famous saying goes, and handing money to our children without requiring effort on their part often creates Money Monsters. Stories of lavish and outlandish spending by children of the rich and famous are constant fodder for entertainment magazines or dramatic headlines that sell newspapers. Yet statistics show[1] that children from relatively affluent homes are afflicted with depression at twice the national rate. Suniya Luthar, Professor of Psychology and Education at Teachers College, Columbia University, attributes this surprising statistic to the use of money and gifts by affluent parents as a substitute for quality time with their children. Such parents often use money to bail their children out of trouble instead of letting them learn the consequences of their actions. These children sometimes suffer from substance abuse and eating disorders, and they often resort to cheating and stealing.

---

1 https://www.psychologytoday.com/articles/201310/the-problem-rich-kids

The most common cause of this problem is the lack of education surrounding money. And parents of every income bracket are guilty of this—they give their children money, without making them work for it, and the children spend it (almost immediately!) without any understanding of where it came from, what it took to get it, and how to use it properly. But this book will show you that the old way is outdated and a new way is here. Imagine your child not asking you for money because they have their own!

Some extremely affluent parents lead by example: they work hard, live modestly, or make demands on their children in order to teach them the value of money. Warren Buffet famously lives in the same little house he bought in 1958. He taught his children the value of a buck by making them earn it and encouraging them to do more. His son, Peter, advocates requiring children to do chores and solve their own problems. *Children learn by example*—if parents aggrandize themselves by accumulating things, the child learns to emulate that behavior.

This is just one example of wealthy parents who didn't allow money to become a substitute for involvement in their children's lives, and who served as living examples of the values that make their children successful today.

You are in the perfect place, at the perfect time, to teach your children the tools that will make them masters not only of their own money, but also of their lives.

Money isn't the root of all evil—the love of money is. It's the root of a lot of confusion and desperation that can turn us into monsters if we search too desperately for ways to get it in order to survive. Its impact on our lives can change our personalities—when we have money, we feel relaxed and in charge; when we don't have money, we feel scared or defeated.

Like any skill, money mastery requires persistence and commitment. Good money habits develop other skills that lead to a well-rounded and fulfilling life. I'm going to show you a simple, fun system to develop these habits. This system, already proven successful with my own sons, will instill discipline and teach your children to take pride in becoming Money Masters.

What Are Money Masters and Money Monsters?

This book is about teaching your child financial and personal self-reliance—being a Money Master—rather than being dependent on others for financial gain and structure—being a Money Monster. Let's look quickly at the two.

MONEY MONSTERS are easy to spot because they're so common. They're created by ignorance, lack of experience, or lack of skills. They come from families across the financial spectrum. Money Monsters look to the world to give them the means to survive. Children are the most common Money Monsters, and their parents are often their creators. Children who constantly nag their parents about buying them things or taking them places without earning such gifts are Money Monsters. They don't understand where money comes from,

1

how long it takes to get it, and what their parents sacrifice to provide it. They repeatedly ask for more and are often rewarded by their parents, who give in to those requests.

Whether they come from a family of wealth or poverty, these children don't understand the value of money and the value of earning their own. With this foundation they can easily grow into oblivious adults who spend instead of save and who throw good money after bad.

If they're wealthy, they have a financial cushion that keeps them safe but doesn't develop them into the fullest people they can be. If they come from poorer families, they live paycheck to paycheck with no financial cushion, at the mercy of the world around them.

What parent wants this for their child?

MONEY MASTERS are those who understand what it takes to earn money, how to save and invest it, and how to develop financial security that protects them until their last days. Parents can make Money Masters of their children while they're young and teachable.

Money Masters not only know how to make money; they understand how to manage it so it works for them. Money Masters will always have enough. Whether they work for themselves or others, they have a system for taking care of the bills, enjoying life, and saving for education or a comfortable retirement.

But such skills aren't natural; they're learned. Like most skills, when they're learned early, they become good habits and build a good life. As Aristotle would aptly put it, "We are what we repeatedly do. Excellence then, is not an act, but a habit." Understanding the banking system helps. Knowing how to identify hidden costs—like taxes—helps. Having experience dealing with the financial market is essential.

When children—like your child—grow up making and managing their own money wisely, they become Money Masters. They can thrive instead of merely survive.

What parent doesn't want this for their child?

Chapter One
Habit #1:
Develop a Money
Master Mindset

Money is earned, not given. Most adults know this, but most children do not. Why? Because they aren't taught it at an early age, and so they have to scramble to understand it later on, when the stakes are high and the rewards are harder to gain. What many adults don't know is this: money mastery begins with our thoughts.

Because children look towards the important people in their lives, and develop thoughts and habits based on what they see and hear, it's important to keep money conversations positive and informative. If they constantly hear those around them talk negatively about finances, they may develop a negative view of money, which in turn creates poor money habits. Parents often say:

- "Money is the root of all evil."
- "We don't have enough money."
- "Rich people are bad because they take advantage of innocent people and they get their money from cheating others."
- "We'll never get rich."
- "Getting rich is a matter of luck or fate."
- "There's not enough to go around for everyone."
—and so on.

We are shaped by our thoughts. We become what we think. Our kids definitely become what they think, and often, they also become what their parents think. As Mahatma Gandhi said, "Your thoughts become your words, your words become your actions, your actions become your habits, your habits become your values, and your values become your destiny." Therefore, it's crucial that we teach our kids to have positive, healthy thoughts about money.

It's never too early to start the conversation—even two-year-olds can begin to understand. Inculcating children with positive attitudes toward money is fundamental to helping them develop the good habits that will make them Money Masters.

Sometimes it takes a reframing process for the parents—especially if they grew up in poor families, as my husband and I did.

As early as age two, my boys began to hear five empowering principles about money that I repeated whenever I felt it was appropriate.

These are:

1. **Money is a vehicle to make our lives comfortable and enjoyable.**

   Never let the pursuit of money become so important that you'll do anything just to have it. Having lots of money is a blessing because it enables us not only to help ourselves and our families, but also to make a difference in other people's lives by sharing. I pointed out to my children how our money makes it possible for us to buy food, get gas for the car, buy a house for our family, or go on trips to celebrate birthdays. Those concrete examples clarified for my sons the connection between having money and living life.

   I volunteer for a non-profit organization that teaches financial literacy to elementary to high-school students in mostly inner-city schools in and around Los Angeles. One day, I was teaching some elementary-school students the first module of the curriculum—what money is and how to get it. One student stood up and said,

7

"Money means everything. It is the main purpose of life and that is what we are living for. I will do whatever it takes to be rich!"

I was surprised that this young mind thought of money in that way, so I asked, "What do you mean by you will do whatever it takes to be rich?"

He said, "That means I don't mind doing some stuff, like bad things."

I was disturbed by his comments, so I asked him, "Who taught you that? Where did you get that idea?" At first, I thought maybe he'd watched too many movies or television dramas, and that these had negatively influenced his mind.

But he replied, "My mom said I should make a lot of money to support the family, and it is okay to do whatever it takes as long as I don't get hurt."

His classmates instantly cheered him, but his attitude concerned me; it seemed to offer a glimpse of what could happen to this boy in the future if he doesn't change his mindset about money and learn the money skills that might change the course of his life.

This elementary schooler was influenced by a mother desperate to support her family. He was taught to approach life with that desperation, and to make

8

money the most important thing in his world—even if getting it might destroy his future. But he was lucky, because he had a chance to learn not just how to "get" money, but how to keep it and build it in ways that won't threaten his life or family. With the right skills, he can help provide for his family without risking everything.

2. Money is everywhere, and there is enough for everyone.

Money is abundant! I told my boys that when God created this world, he created everything abundantly, including money. There is enough money to go around for everyone who works hard and smart, works wisely for themselves and for others—regardless of their social status, ethnicity, religious background, or where they live.

There are about seven billion people in this world as of 2015, and the world's wealth totals more than $60 trillion dollars! A trillion is equal to a thousand billions (1,000 x 1,000,000,000). That's a lot of money! Some people say, "There is too much money in too few hands." But that money mentality comes from a perception of scarcity, not abundance. There's plenty for all of us if we learn to tame the Money Monster in us and turn it into a Money Master.

3. Money is good and useful.

I really wanted to drill into my sons' minds that it's good to have money—lots of money. Money is not the root of evil, but the *love* of money is, according to the Bible. In my profession as a financial advisor, I've met many multi-millionaires who love giving and sharing.

To teach that the goodness of money lies in the hands of the person who has it, I often use this example: If a chef has a knife, he makes great food, and if a surgeon has a knife, he saves other people's lives. But if a criminal has a knife, he can harm others, and if a child has a knife, he can harm himself. It isn't the money itself that determines whether it is good or bad, but the person who decides how to get that money and how to use it.

4. You become rich by adding value to others.

My boys and I often listened to the late Jim Rohn's great motivational speeches about money. In one of his seminars, he said, "We get paid for bringing value to the marketplace. It takes time, but we get paid for the value, not the time." My sons often imitated how he said this, and they laughed. But they *heard* him.

Following Rohn's philosophy of adding value, I taught them that if our work adds more value to more people, we make more money. Less value equals less money. It's not by stepping on other people's toes that we get rich, but by helping them to get what they want in life.

5. Share it with others

This is a very difficult concept for children to grasp at first, especially if they do not see their parents practice what they preach. Many adults fail to appreciate how profoundly sharing with others benefits the one who shares. But a generous, compassionate role model can make it easy for your child to understand this.

I give lots of credit to my husband, Thomas, a loving and giving man whose day-to-day life is a great example to my boys of how to share with others. One hot summer day, our whole family was walking down the street when we saw a young pregnant woman sitting in front of a store, begging. She was wearing dirty, ragged clothing and seemed very tired and hungry. Some people didn't even bother to look at her, or they just glanced at her and walked right past.

The minute Thomas saw her, he stopped. Our boys were holding his hands, but their eyes opened wide when he asked, "Young lady, are you hungry?"

Her face showed her fatigue when she answered, "Yes."

As soon as she said that, Thomas took the boys with him into a pizza place inside the store where he bought a whole combo pizza with a drink. When he gave them to her, she was surprised and immediately thanked him.

I watched the whole scene. Afterward, I smiled and asked him, "How come you didn't just give her some money instead?" He said, "I was sure that she was hungry and needed food, but I wasn't sure that giving her money in that situation would benefit her. There was a chance that she might misuse the money by spending it on something bad that might harm her and her baby." Jason and Matthew listened to every word. They were so proud of their dad—and I was, too.

We do not do any service nor add any value to life by being poor. When we are poor and can't support ourselves, we become a financial burden to our families, our community, and our world at large.

However, many of us never have enough money, even if we have jobs that pay us enough to live, because it slips like sand through our fingers. If no one has taught us how to manage money, this neglected lesson can turn into a lifelong struggle that robs us of the fulfilling experience of being able to give—as Thomas gave food to that woman.

Everywhere we turn, we are bombarded by promotions for easy ways to get rich and by enticements to buy more things and to have the best and the biggest. And to do it *fast*. But fast is not the way most successes happen. They happen over time, day by day, with sustained and focused effort. Success requires self-discipline, dedication, and looking toward the future.

For many of us, success equals having lots of money. Lack of money often leads to low self-esteem, a growing sense of futility, and resentment toward those who seem—almost magically—to have not only enough, but more than enough money to live their lives in comfort and safety.

Earning our own money and controlling what happens to it builds confidence that we are in charge of our lives, even if we work for someone else. When we walk out the door and into the bank or the brokerage company with our bucks, we are the Money Masters who determine how much money stays and how much goes. We may not all be millionaires, but all of us can see the positive results of earning, saving, investing, and spending wisely. And it's never too early to begin.

Possession of anything begins in our minds, with our thoughts. As Gandhi said, our thoughts become our habits. Getting clear on our priorities, focusing on an attitude of abundance, and being grateful for every opportunity to reach our goals makes our thoughts our first money-mastery tool.

When you give your children money, tell them, "This money is like a seed. If you plant it now and take great care of it, it will grow into a BIG tree in your future. You can do it because you are a Money Master!" Your children will begin to think of themselves and their money in a positive way—and this is the first building block of success.

THE TAKEAWAY

Our thoughts are the first tool in our Money Master toolbox. Make your child's first experiences with money positive and healthy.

Chapter Two

Habit #2:
Start Saving Early!

Sow the seeds of saving habits early.

Samuel Smiles once said, "Sow a thought, and you reap an act; sow an act, and you reap a habit; sow a habit, and you reap a character; sow a character, and you reap a destiny."

When I became a mother, the idea that we reap what we sow intrigued me and I wanted to make sure I sowed the right kind of thought and the right kind of action into my boys' early lives. I wanted the seeds of good money principles like "The soul of the diligent is richly supplied" deeply planted in their minds.

Every time they asked me to buy them things, even when they were as young as two-years-old, my answer was, "You don't ask for money. Think about what you can do to earn the money to buy that yourself."

To help them accomplish this, I encouraged them to do age-appropriate chores at home—emptying the trash bags, raking leaves, watering the plants, folding the laundry… They may have been only a few years old, but even a two- or three-year-old can water a plant or fold their own socks. I didn't expect them to do it perfectly; I expected them to do it to the best of their ability and with a good attitude.

To help them see how work earns money, I bought them a ceramic cow bank. After they did a couple of chores, I gave them coins to put into it. Small children are easily delighted, and my sons loved dropping the coins into their little bank. At this age, coins always work better than bills. Coins are easier for little fingers to grasp, play with, and drop into piggy banks, and their weight adds importance in a young mind that paper doesn't. My sons received one dollar a week in coins. As they dropped them into their little cow bank, I counted, "Five pennies, three nickels, three dimes, and two quarters …" They loved that—it sounded like so much money!

Into the bank clinked the coins. Day by day, the cow got heavier. They checked it out, slid the coins around, laughed, and joked with each other about it. I loved listening to them talk about "their cow bank" and "their money." You could hear excitement and pride in their voices!

My young boys learned to anticipate getting money for a job well done, and that delighted me. Jason and Matthew were not only acquiring coins, but also growing in unseen but more crucial ways—in self-confidence, pride, and discipline. They learned that doing a job well and with a good attitude is satisfying and inspiring, and that they are in charge of their actions, decisions, and outlooks. For me, this is the deepest meaning of "being rich" and becoming a "Money Master."

Piggy—The Young Money Master's First Bank

I eventually realized something about that first ceramic cow bank—they couldn't see anything inside it. So when it was time to get more serious about teaching them about money, I wanted them to each have their own *small* and *transparent* piggy bank that they could see. These two characteristics are important to feeding a child's sense of accomplishment and success.

In our case, my sons chose two different piggy banks. Actually, neither was a pig—one looked like a frog and the other was a panda bear. Choosing their own banks gave them a sense of ownership about what went into them.

*Their first frog and panda bear banks. This was
where they began saving their college funds!*

A transparent bank helps a child see the reality of what's happening. We all want to see the results of our efforts, and this is especially true for young children who don't have the ability to imagine the future yet. When your children can see the coins drop in, pile on top of one another, and move around, they understand cause and effect—doing your chores well causes your bank to fill.

The banks have to be small so they will fill up fast. Week by week, as they dropped their allowances in, my boys watched the pile of coins inside grow until it reached all the way to the top of the frog's or panda's head. Of course, they talked about their banks and played around with them to hear the coins move. The tactile delight of swishing the coins or feeling the increasing weight of the banks gave my sons a lot of pleasure. They dreamed and schemed about what they would do with their money. And the success of seeing their money increase inspired them to keep going.

As parents, our word is our promise. This is *so* important to remember. When we promise something, immediate action has to follow. When I told my sons that their money would soon fill their banks, they had to be able to see it happen—fast. Small piggy banks (or frog or bear or cow banks) make a big impression on your child because the pile of quarters and dimes quickly reaches the top.

First the coins reached up to the feet, then the belly, then the neck, the chin, and the head. When it was all the way up to the ears, we took it to the bank. At this stage, it is very important that parents *do not* use or touch their coins *at all.* For your child to feel in control of their money, they need to be the only one handling it. If you do this for them, they will learn at a young age that *somebody* else will handle their money, get discouraged from doing it themselves, and they may not learn the habit of saving.

Paper Wallets for Paper Money

When my boys advanced from kindergarten to first grade, I increased their weekly allowance from one dollar to two dollars a week. I gave them both coins and paper money. Because they were now getting paper money, we rolled the dollar bills so they were easy to remove without tearing them.

By now they understood that paper money was worth as much as coins or more. They needed wallets where they could put their spending money, so I devised a paper wallet that we made together.

Why make a wallet with paper? Buying our children wallets from a store is much easier and faster, but by doing so we miss the opportunity to create a great memory that will last your child's lifetime. Your children will always remember their first wallets that they made with their mommy or daddy, as my boys do. If you think paper is too delicate, let me tell you that my sons had their first wallets for four years! Just last year, I made new ones for them; later they bought "real" wallets, like their dad's ... with their own money.

So, one Saturday morning, we all sat around the table to make those first paper wallets. On the table were several pieces of blank white paper, scissors, and Scotch tape. If your child is

20

old enough, they can construct their wallet themselves. Here's how to make the world's simplest wallet:

1. Fold a piece of paper horizontally (lengthwise) in half; then unfold it.
2. Fold each short side toward the other until they meet in the center. Don't unfold.
3. Fold the paper horizontally in half again. This creates two layers of paper that make the wallet strong and create two compartments.
4. Tape the short sides securely so the money won't slip out.
5. Decorate!

Kids love creating things, especially things they can use. My boys loved the whole process and were excited to have their very own wallets. When their paper wallets were made, they each breathed their unique personalities into them—Jason drew a Pokémon with color pens and crayons, and Matthew drew some creative figures from his imagination.

While they were decorating their wallets, I told them that 10 percent of the money they earned was to be given to God, and out of the remaining 90 percent, 50 percent of the money was to go into the wallet for spending, and the other 50 percent was to go into their piggy banks to be saved for college. I just wanted to keep the rules as simple as possible for them to follow at that age, but later adopted a more complicated allocation method. They both wanted to go to Princeton because I'd told them Princeton has a great basketball team, and my boys *love* basketball—the idea of playing basketball for Princeton inspired them to tuck away those dollars!

"When you go to great schools like Harvard, Princeton, or Yale, you can get a scholarship if you do well, and the school may even pay for your school expenses," I said. "Then you can use all your savings for something else!"

"You mean ... like buying a car?" Jason asked.

"Or you mean, like buying DS?" Matthew giggled, knowing that I thought Nintendo games like DS were a waste of money.

We laughed and had a lot of fun while they decorated their wallets. When they'd finished, they took the spending

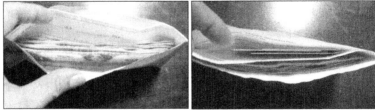

The mighty wallet stuffed with cash

portion of their allowance and proudly put it into their brand new wallets. Now they had money in a wallet, just like dad.

Someone once said, "Life is not measured by the number of breaths we take, but by the moments that take our breath away."[1] I absolutely agree. Something as simple as hanging out with your children while they decorate their first wallets and dream of what that money will do is one of those moments in life that will take your breath away—and those are the moments that count! As parents, we know that these moments are fleeting. When my boys are older and have leather wallets that hold credit cards, I will always remember the hilarity and closeness we shared as we all made their first paper wallets together. And so will they.

Making paper wallets with your children helps them engage in this money matter, encouraging them to stay disciplined, to plan ahead, and to feel a sense of accomplishment. It's a fun way to show them that they are doing something for their future, even with these small steps. Splitting their money into tithing, saving and spending accounts shows your children how easy it is to manage their money and to balance their budgets. Here's what else it does: it motivates them to earn more bucks (or credits—more about that later) by doing more chores.

---

1 Hillary Cooper. http://www.globaleducationconference.com/profiles/blogs/life-is-not-measured-by-the

Piggy's First Trip to the Local Bank

In the early years, we are our children's first teachers and most important role models. I believe our primary role as parents is to prepare our children for the future, for the BIG real world out there. To us, it may feel like a journey of a thousand miles, but it all starts with a single step and continues one step at a time—and this is especially true of personal finance.

Now that the boys had piggy banks and wallets, it became a habit for them to save money and keep it in their piggy banks. They used the money in their wallets to buy things for themselves or others, and brought the money in their piggy banks—both coins and dollar bills—to deposit in the local bank. (They are still using their little banks. Right now, each of them has saved about $100 toward college—money that will soon go into their bank accounts.) When their piggy banks got full, I told my boys that they'd saved so much, there was no more room for any more coins or bills. We needed to move their money somewhere else, somewhere *safer*—a local bank.

Some parents may think that kids six years old or younger cannot understand complex financial matters, but *trust me*, they do. Our kids are much smarter than we think. At first, the boys didn't understand why their piggy-bank money had to be moved to a place where they couldn't see it every day.

I explained to them that the bank is a place to keep people's money safe, and that it also pays those account holders extra money, which it puts into their savings accounts. "That extra money is called *interest*," I said. "Interest is free money that the bank gives to you, like a bonus for your good work." Once they had a picture in their mind of that free money, they sure liked the idea!

I had them choose their local bank, and they chose a different bank from the one their parents used. They called it "My Bank." For the first few visits to "their bank," I filled out the deposit slip and explained the process of filling it out, step by step, as they watched. First, we counted the money together. Then, while they watched, I wrote on the slip the date, account number, and the amount they would deposit. They brought the deposit slips and piggy banks to the banker.

To some children, it can be very sad to watch as all their money goes away and their piggy banks come back empty. My boys were sad too, at first. After the first deposit, they didn't even want to hold their empty piggy banks! With his eyes full of tears, Jason asked, "Mommy, you said that they would give us more money—interest—but there is no money in here!"

So I showed them the receipt and pointed out where it said how much they'd deposited that day and what their current balance was. Jason wasn't convinced, so we all went back to the bank teller who'd helped them.

Bank tellers can be your allies as your children develop this "save now" habit. Tell them that you're teaching your daughter or son about money management and saving, and ask them to help you encourage your child.

When I explained that the boys needed proof that they hadn't lost their money, she kindly gave them a deposit receipt, on the back of which she had written the balance from today's deposit. She reassured them, saying, "Your money is safely deposited into your account, and you will get interest sometime soon. Don't worry." And then she gave them lollipops. Hearing the teller say their money was safe made the difference, even if it hadn't earned any interest yet. Sometimes, the best reassurance comes from an authority figure they don't know.

Luckily for us, the bank also provided free hot chocolate. For my sons, sitting on the bank couch and drinking hot chocolate sweetened what had been a slightly confusing experience.

We continued to make regular visits to "their" local bank. Soon they were able to write their own deposit slips. Each time, they checked the savings account box, wrote the date, account number, and the dollar amount, and brought it to the teller with their money. I told them that they were way ahead of the game, because most young children don't even *have* bank accounts, much less know how to write their own deposit slips. This made them feel *very* grown up and proud.

The local bankers were surprised by what we were doing, but they really liked it. New lifelong customers were in the making! I appreciated the bankers' enthusiasm, and many of them cooperated with me. They were very supportive of the idea that I was helping my sons establish good saving habits. Not only did the tellers understand, but they went the extra mile for my boys. Many said things like, "Wow, you guys are doing great! I am very proud of you for saving for your future at this young age. You will be very successful and rich when you grow up!" There's nothing like compliments to boost a child's confidence!

Every time they deposited money at their local bank, the boys wanted to drink something like hot chocolate, and they wanted me to enjoy coffee or tea from there, too. They seemed to think that every time they deposited money, we had earned the privilege to take advantage of the free drinks. One day, we stopped by their bank to get some information about their accounts. Jason wanted to drink hot chocolate as usual, but Matthew stopped him, saying, "No, Jason. We have to *earn* that hot chocolate. We need to bring our deposit first and then drink it."

Jason said, "You're right. We didn't bring our money!"

With those words, they showed me how much they'd learned about saving money. They learned the reason for the bank, their work, how saving can equal future benefits, and what it means to earn a reward. It was a proud mommy moment!

The cool thing was that every time we came back from their bank, they were eager to earn extra money by doing more chores at home. By now, they were almost six years old and could do harder tasks. So when they did chores like vacuuming the living room, dusting the furniture, watering the plants, trimming the leaves, cleaning their room, washing the dishes, or just assisting me at dinnertime, I gave them extra incentives.

Now that they were looking for more ways to help and earn extra money, I had to come up with a plan. That's how the Morning Stuff allowance was born. But that Morning Stuff allowance ended up being so much more than just a way to earn money—it ended up being a positive thing for them *and* me, every single day.

Life is like catching fish, right? From the beginning, we need to learn the skills that we'll use to survive and create our lives—to catch the fish we want. Through the Morning Stuff allowance, my kids learned how to catch fish on their own, instead of relying on me to give it to them.

THE TAKEAWAY

Give your child these powerful tools of money mastery—a piggy bank and a paper wallet. Then take them to the bank or the credit union, and open an account with them so they learn to navigate the banking system.

Chapter Three

Habit #3:
Create Reminders,
Routines, and Rewards

The Morning Stuff Allowance Project

How many mommies or daddies in this world get to hear their young children say every morning, "Mommy, Daddy, wake up! It's time to get up!" I bet not many. Fortunately, I was one of those few lucky moms.

Normally, it's the other way around, right? Moms (or dads) go to their kids' rooms and do whatever they can to wake them up and to get them ready for school. Kids hate it.

They stay in bed, complain, and only do half of what they need to do to get out the door and to school on time. They forget to brush their teeth or to take the stuff they need for the day. They yell or whine. They don't eat breakfast, and then an hour later they can't concentrate because their blood sugar is at zero and they don't have enough energy. Mentally, mornings are often a bloody battle between parents and their children. How tiring!

Morning is the busiest and most important time of the day, and we parents need to be supercharged so that we are not dragged down by poor attitudes. This is especially true for working moms—me included. We do not have the luxury of unlimited time to watch our children and take care of chores when time permits. If we did that, we'd be late for work!

Not only is this an unproductive way to begin a day, but by doing so, we can also miss out on great bonding time with our children. Simply having breakfast together, going over the plans for the day, or just saying a few words to encourage our kids before they go to school makes *all* the difference. But the sad reality is that we often hurry through our mornings with our children.

Every day is a day that will never happen again. Even though you may know that there are many years of parenting still to come, with each year that passes, you still look back and marvel, "Where did the time go?" Each morning with our children can be a sharing time … if we don't have to fight the morning battles.

Mornings don't have to be a struggle any longer. Let me show you the simple solution that has worked so well for our family. It's an incentive-reward system that I came up with many years ago for myself and my children, and it's still going *very* strong. I never imagined how much they'd embrace it—even five years later! As I write this book, my boys are entering middle school. We are still using this system every day, and it's a win-win solution for all of us.

When they were still in kindergarten moving into first grade, I needed to come up with a plan that would reward my boys for their good works *and* create stress-free mornings for all of us. That's how my "Morning Stuff Allowance" reward system was created.

As I said earlier, I designed this system for two reasons. First, I wanted to spend my morning time with my boys as productively, peacefully, and lovingly as possible. And second, I wanted to create more ways to give them incentives, credits, and legitimately hard-earned money to reward their good work and good behavior.

So, one day I sat down with them and introduced the Morning Stuff Allowance idea. I told them that I would give them more allowance when they did their morning stuff all by themselves, without me reminding them or saying *Ppali Ppali* (which means "hurry, hurry" in Korean). Of course they asked, "What is the morning stuff, Mommy?"

"Nothing special," I said. "It's just doing the stuff you do in the morning!" When they looked at me, confused, I explained. "It's very simple. You get up at 6:30 when the alarm clock rings and make your beds, get dressed, eat breakfast, put your lunch box and water bottle into your school bag, use the restroom, and so on!"

After listening carefully, Jason asked, "So ... if we do all these things, how much do we get?"

"THREE dollars!" I said with a big smile, putting a huge accent on "three."

"Three ... dollars?" Matthew responded, unconvinced.

"Yes! Not only that, you will also get bonuses and special project incentives, too! So if you do all of these, you can make a lot of money, *easily*."

By now, they were convinced. "Okay, Mommy. Let's do it!"

It's important for parents to set simple rules that are easy for children to understand and follow. Our children are not robots, and they are willing to do anything to please their parents when they feel loved and cared for. By explaining that they are in charge of earning their own money by doing familiar jobs that they are confident they can do, you initiate a conversation instead of laying down rules and demands that do little but invite rebellion. Giving your children the chance to be powerful in one area of their lives teaches them to take charge in *all* aspects of their lives. This sense of autonomy and choice will empower them during the difficult teen years, when most kids are susceptible to peer pressure and run the risk of making bad choices.

The night after we made the deal, I picked their clothing out and put it next to their beds, and we all went to sleep.

The next morning came. Jason and Matthew didn't wake up on time. When the alarm clock rang at 6:30 a.m., one of the boys turned it off and they went back to sleep. I waited until almost 7:00 a.m. before going into their room and whispering into their ears quietly, "It's past 6:30. Remember your morning s-t-u-f-f?"

The moment they heard the words "morning stuff," they sprang out of bed and began doing their morning preparations. They made their beds, got dressed, ate their breakfast, packed their backpacks, brushed their teeth, and got ready for school at around 7:40 a.m.

I'm not saying it was perfect from the get-go; it wasn't. But it was a good start. From that day until now, our mornings have been struggle-free.

Morning Stuff Allowance Chart

The first week wasn't as smooth as I'd expected, but they made it through and finally got used to the routine. To help us keep track of the activities for the next four weeks, I drew a simple Morning Stuff Allowance chart and put it on the wall in our dining area.

		May 20		May 27		June 3		June 10	
		Time	chores	T	C	T	C	T	C
Jason M	Typing	7:00	Trash	7:05	M2171	7:00	T	7:00	sweep
Matthew	creating	7:00	T	7:05	trush	7:00	T	7:00	M21
J	Book	7:09	T	''	T	7:10	T	7:09	T
M	Report	7:14	T	6:59	T	7:10	T	7:08	T
J	Drawing	6:51	T	7:00	T	7:05	T	6:59	''
M	Read Tup	''	+	6:59	T	7:07	T	6:52	''
J	Book	6:59	T	6:57	T	7:20	T	6:59	''
M	Report	7:00	T	7:00	T	7:11	T	7:01	''
J	Movie	6:55	T	7:03	T	7:05	T	7:15	''
M		6:55	T	7:03	T	7:05	F	6:59	T
J	Book								
M	project								

Our first Morning Stuff Allowance Chart

Check out what this chart contains: the date, their names, daily special activities, chores, and the time they completed that chore. Letting your child fill out the chart increases their sense of ownership of the project. It helps make them responsible *to themselves.* And with the chart on display, everyone can see how much they have accomplished, which is a form of public affirmation.

Ever since we put this allowance system in place, our typical morning has gone like this:

- Jason and Matthew get up at 6:30 when the alarm clock rings
- They make their beds nicely
- They put on the clothing that I prepare the night before
- They pack their backpacks to get ready for school
- They eat breakfast—a healthy bowl of cereal and fruit
- They bring the breakfast dishes and utensils to the sink
- They wash their faces and brush their teeth
- They leave for school before 7:30 a.m.

If they completed each of these tasks every day, from Monday through Friday, they got three dollars on Saturday morning. Jason and Matthew could claim this money *only when* they finished all their morning stuff. If they missed one or two, or didn't do well on any of these activities (either due to incompletion or *bad attitude*), I gave them a small deduction point, like 10 cents on each activity. They didn't like the deduction! Of course, nobody likes negative consequences.

After the first couple of weeks, they tried hard to get things done quickly. They did their morning chores, like emptying the trash bag (T or 쓰레기 in Korean on the chart indicates

Trash) or sweeping the front yard before going to school. And they wrote the time of completion on the chart when they were done. Most of the time, they were able to finish everything by around 7:00 a.m.

Do you think that sounds like a fantasy? It isn't, and my sons ended up loving this system.

It became like a competition between my two boys to see who could finish first each morning. They moved quickly— from dining room to restroom, from the restroom to their room, from here to there—to get things done as fast as possible. Many times, it made me laugh to watch them and to listen to them egging each other on.

Every family is different in what they need or want from their children, so your Morning Stuff Allowance chart will probably be different from ours. Be creative and work together with your children. Set achievable goals so that your children accomplish what you need them to accomplish and can feel proud of their own efforts.

Peter Andrew Buffett is an Emmy Award-winning musician and author, as well as the youngest son of the world-famous billionaire investor Warren Buffett. In his book, *Life Is What You Make It,* he says, "As kids, we didn't take anything for granted. I received a small allowance, but it wasn't simply handed to me; I earned it." In his advice to parents, he talks about the importance of requiring children to do chores and letting them solve problems on their own instead of bailing them out.

If your house is nothing but chaos in the morning, maybe you have to begin with just a couple of chores. Make the reward small but inspiring. As the days or weeks go by and your kids get better at doing this, gradually increase what they need to get done so they can earn more. Later, when they're older or just wanting to earn more money, you can add more chores that they can do in the morning or after school. Some of these chores can include emptying the trash bags, sweeping the floor, dusting, putting toys and books away, bringing in the mail, vacuuming, mopping the floor, watering plants and flowers, raking leaves, dishwashing, sorting laundry, setting the table, pet walking, washing the car, and babysitting (if they're old enough).

Put the chart in the place that gets the most traffic in your home. In ours, that's the dining room area, where we gather to eat, do homework, and have family meetings. Having the chart in this room meant that everybody could see it, all the time, and it reinforced the boys progress in their minds. They began to feel good about watching the chart fill up with check-off times, my signatures (I added this column later, when I made a few changes), and the chores they accomplished every week.

In his blog post, "The 3 R's of Habit Change: How to Start New Habits That Actually Stick," James Clear says this:

Your life today is essentially the sum of your habits from the past ... How successful or unsuccessful you are [is a] result of your habits.[1]

Clear explains how every habit has the same three-step pattern: a *Reminder* that initiates the behavior; a *Routine*, which is the behavior itself; and the *Reward* that is gained from doing the behavior.

Charles Duhigg, author of *The Power of Habit,* tells how MIT researchers discovered a simple neurological loop at the core of every habit, a loop that consists of three parts: *A cue, a routine and a reward.* This is essentially the same thing that Clear says above.

In our case, the reminder or the cue is the "Morning Stuff Allowance" system; the routine is doing all the morning stuff every day *with a good attitude*; and the reward is receiving three dollars, plus bonuses and incentives.

"What we repeatedly do ultimately forms the person we are, the things we believe, and the personality that we portray," Clear says in his article, and I couldn't agree more. This Morning Stuff Allowance is not only generating extra money

---

1 http://jamesclear.com/three-steps-habit-change

for my boys, but also helping them form new, empowering habits that will pay off throughout their lifetimes.

At first, it was effort*ful,* but later it became so effort*less* that even if they forgot to turn on their alarm clock the night before, they were on autopilot and were still able to get up on time to do their morning stuff.

Every day there are different activities, but the key to it all is that every job *must* have a reward. Remember the last of the three patterns to reinforce a good habit? Our brains love rewards!

Parents often make the mistake of forcing our children to do too many things. We take them to soccer practice, football games, tae kwon do class, art class, ballet lessons, and so on. We think it's good for our children's development, and that we are fulfilling our parental duty.

But structured activities (even fun ones) are a requirement on a child's energy and time, just like a job is. Most of the time, we forget to *reward* our children for their work, for putting in the effort to practice! We forget to *celebrate* small or big accomplishments. Rewards have tremendous impacts that make your child feel recognized and appreciated. Give them a monetary reward, buy something they've wanted for a long time, or go watch a movie or eat yummy food together.

How can we make the new habits last forever? Rewards! The beauty of a reward is that it doesn't have to be big. It has to be consistent and appropriate to the efforts of the child. If your budget is tight, make the reward fit your budget. It's the recognition that matters most.

On top of monetary rewards, my boys also received huge applause and compliments from my husband and me, which is a powerful psychological and emotional reward. It's the easiest reinforcement for a parent to give, but praise is no small thing. Children thrive on positive reinforcement. When they get it, they repeat the actions that earned it. When they don't get it, they are defeated, frustrated, confused, or angry. None of these emotions will encourage them to stick to the system. Be sure to reward your child, not just with money, but with praise.

The Special Incentive Project

Something that went very well with Morning Stuff Allowance was the Special Incentive Project. The "Special Incentive Project" is something extra your children can do on top of their already existing regular daily or weekly activities. Instead of going through the same routine day in and day out, you can actually design ahead of time how you want the days to look for your children, and have lots of fun with it. Again, this is something extra you would add to their regular weekly activities.

Here's how the Special Incentive Project looked for Jason and Matthew when we first adopted this idea: Monday, typing practice and creativity work; Tuesday, book project; Wednesday, drawing and reading; Thursday, book project; and Friday, movie night. This chart below is one of my early ones that worked for us until I made a few changes later on. Here I added a Parents Signature and Bonus Work column in the chart. This chart can be downloaded from the website www.nomoneymonster.com.

Morning Stuff Allowance Chart with Special Incentive Project					
Day of the Week (Special Incentive P)	Wake-Up Time	Completion Time	Daily Chores	Parents Signature	Bonus Works
Monday (Typing Practice & Creativity)	6:30 AM	7:10 AM	Empting Trash	Sign	Watering
Tuesday (Book Report)	6:30 AM	7:10 AM	Sweeping	Sign	Empting Trash
Wednesday (Drawing & Reading)	6:30 AM	7:10 AM	Empting Trash	Sign	Helping cooking
Thursday (Book Report)	6:30 AM	7:10 AM	Sweeping	Sign	Massage
Friday (Fun Movie Night)	6:30 AM	7:10 AM	Empting Trash	Sign	Folding Laundry
Saturday (Korean School & Sports & Ceremony)	7:30AM	Your Choice	Your Choice	Sign	Your Choice
Sunday (Church & Free Time)	8:00AM	Your Choice	Your Choice	Sign	Your Choice

The Amazing Book Project

Out of all the Special Incentive Projects I had for my boys, I particularly liked the book projects they did on Tuesdays and Thursdays. I called it the "Amazing Book Project." I said, "If you read more than two hundred books, Mommy will get you the puppy you want when we move to a new house."

"Really, Mommy?" they asked. Their excited faces lit up with huge smiles and glowing cheeks.

For the Amazing Book Project, we borrowed many, MANY books from the local library. At each visit, they borrowed up to thirty books per library card—a total of sixty books—and brought them home. I challenged them: "Read something that will stimulate your brain, not something too easy."

When they were selecting their books for the coming month or so, they often asked "Mommy, is this book too easy?"

They did three book reports each week, and each report had an introduction, a body, and a conclusion. I needed to draw a book project chart that was separate from the Morning Stuff Allowance chart. Every time they finished their book reports, I read them, wrote some comments, and put stamps on the date, along with the title of the book on the right-hand column.

Because Jason and Matthew made frequent visits to the library and borrowed so many books, the head librarian recognized them and gave them awards and cool library bags.

Five book report charts put together in our dining room

By the time they were in the third grade, they had finished more than two hundred book reports, so their third-grade teacher—who also had read all of their previous reports—decided to give them full credit for the reading she required in class. Jason and Matthew, therefore, didn't have to participate in the class reading projects—but they participated in the projects anyway, regardless of the credit. They were "double-dipping" in the best of ways!

So what was their reward for the Amazing Book Project?

When I first introduced them to the idea of doing a book report as part of their Special Incentive Project, I promised them that they would get *twenty dollars* each month upon successful completion, or they could use the twenty-dollar credit for the movie of their choice at the movie theater. They could also have a large popcorn and a drink of their choice! They liked the idea because, until then, we hardly ever went to a movie theater.

Was this book project on top of their three-dollar Morning Stuff Allowance *and* the extra money for their chores and bonus work? Yes! So, it was an exciting deal for them.

Matthew holding one of the many book report charts

"When Mommy makes a promise, Mommy keeps it!" This mantra is frequently repeated in our home, so they were confident that I would do what I said. And I did. Since the

Amazing Book Project was born, many years ago, my husband and I have watched many animated movies with them at the movie theater. We are experts on *Tangled, Toy Story 3, Kung Fu Panda 2, How to Train Your Dragon, The Lego Movie* and so on. You name it, we've seen it.

Saturday Morning Stuff Celebration

Practice small wins? Yes!

Charles Duhigg said that allowing ourselves to appreciate our accomplishments wires our brains to expect positive outcomes. That means we get to celebrate our children's small wins in physical, emotional, and psychological ways, and that's what we did every Saturday morning. I called it the "Morning Stuff Celebration."

After having breakfast together, we sat around the dining table and I asked my boys, "So, did you do all the morning stuff this week?"

"Yes!" they said.

"Great job!" I said. "The chart shows that it's completed. Did you do everything with a good attitude?"

"Yes!" they replied.

"Great job," I told them. "Because you did such a wonderful job this week, *Appa* (Korean for 'Dad') and Mommy would like to present this money to you as a reward." Then I handed three dollars to each of them.

I also gave them some additional bonuses and incentives. When they did extra bonus work such as taking out the trash and watering the plants three times a week, I gave them each an extra dollar. And if they did it four times, I gave them yet another dollar. Lots of bucks!

You can imagine how happy they were. They felt like kings, and that made them even more dedicated to doing their morning stuff, their Special Incentive Project, *and* their bonus work.

And that's the point, isn't it? When we reward small accomplishments or actions, it drives us to do something bigger (to get a bigger accomplishment!). In life, we usually start small to win big. We begin at the beginner's level to become masters of our lives, our goals, and our values. Learning at a young age that effort produces rewards prepares us to become masterful with our money, time, and energy.

Every time I handed the money to one of them, the rest of the family clapped, wore big smiles, and said, "Great job! You did it!" Participating in the celebration of another person's accomplishment teaches us to be generous. If your children know that they will also be recognized and appreciated, they will enjoy encouraging others. I am sure that this kind of celebration will have a positive impact on your children. Your children need to know, feel, and sense that their works are appreciated and that their parents are proud of them.

My sons are now ten years old, almost eleven. So what has happened since these two projects—the Morning Stuff Allowance and Special Incentive Project—were instituted in our home?

Everything in life changes and grows, so I've made a few more changes here and there in the Morning Stuff Allowance and Special Incentive Project systems. The allowance grew from three dollars when they were six years old to five dollars when they were seven, and to seven dollars when they were ten years old on top of their bonuses and incentives. Along with each allowance increase came increased responsibility and increased activities.

Even after almost five years, their morning routines haven't changed much, and I can see that my boys have learned not only how to take care of themselves in the morning, but also how to save, spend, and manage money. They've learned time management and self-discipline. By participating in the Amazing Book Project, they developed better reading and writing skills, they learned about sports, science, and nature, and they've discovered all the great people in human history who overcame difficulties and became successful.

But the most important thing that has changed over the years is how they view the money—it's actually *their* money—and how they share it with others. When they were just seven years old, they worked hard and received five dollars a week. One of their goals at that time was to buy their dad the NBA basketball video game *2K12* for Christmas. This game was very popular among their friends—even their uncle had it—so they wanted to buy it for their dad. And they did it. At the end of the year, they had saved enough money to buy the game for their dad and a nice rainbow bracelet for their mommy.

How sweet! I vividly remember how proud they were of themselves, and I could see how good they felt about giving the gifts … That was one of their early lessons in the joy of sharing affluence. I'll tell you more about it later on.

So what happened to the puppy? Confession here: My boys finished two hundred books a long, long time ago—actually, they had completed more than a thousand book reports by the time they finished the fourth grade. But I haven't bought them a puppy yet. Why? Because we haven't yet moved into a house big enough to have a pet running around. But when we move, I will buy them a puppy—because they earned it, and because when Mommy makes a promise, she keeps it!

THE TAKEAWAY

Reminders, Routines, and Rewards are a surefire way to establish positive habits that last a lifetime.

Chapter Four

Habit #4:
Set High Goals Through
Expectations

Over the past five years, Jason and Matthew had worked so diligently on the Morning Stuff and the Special Incentive Project that they had grown tremendously in the areas of saving, spending wisely, investing for future, contributing to the family, and sharing money with others.

As a mom, I wouldn't trade any of those experiences with them for anything in the world! Every effort they made during those years has become a golden stepping stone for their future success.

However, success can be also a breeding ground for complacency that ultimately breeds failure. Ever since we'd moved to our new home (not big enough for a pet) in Rancho Palos Verdes, California, I could sense the danger of complacency in them when they saw they could almost effortlessly do the same things day in and day out to get the promised rewards.

I believe that complacency is our biggest enemy. When we are comfortable with the status quo we become complacent; we no longer strive to do our best, and therefore we stop growing. That is the beginning of a tragedy.

Benjamin E. Mays, an influential minister, once said "The tragedy of life is often not in our failure, but rather in our complacency; not in our doing too much, but rather in our doing too little; not in our living above our ability, but rather in our living below our capacities."[1]

We all want our children to succeed in life and continue to grow, not only physically, but also spiritually, mentally, emotionally—in every aspect of their lives. We do not want our children to be stuck at the fifth-grade level for life.

I am not a Tiger Mom, but I want the best for my children. So when I sensed that my sons were sailing along in their comfort zone, I needed to do something about it. I shook their

---

1 http://www.brainyquote.com/quotes/quotes/b/benjamine610662. html

52

world upside down and challenged them to set higher goals by kicking it up another notch with a brand new project!

I spent a lot of time trying to figure out how to challenge my boys and inspire them to reach higher, and "The Journey to Greatness" was born.

Why call it a "Journey to Greatness"? Because I believe that we are constantly on the journey to greatness in our lives. Really successful people have struggled through the same process that my boys were just beginning.

For my boys, I used the example of a growing tree to illustrate how life is a continuous process of personal growth. "Every tree wants to be the mightiest, tallest tree in the forest," I explained. As I talked, I drew a picture of a fully grown tree and encouraged them to contribute to it, drawing small birds and fruits. Listening while drawing gave the lesson two ways to sink into their minds—a kinetic way and an intellectual one.

"Trees," I said, "don't grow half way and say to themselves, 'I have grown enough now and am going to stop growing and just relax.' No! They grow their roots as deep as they can, stretch their branches as high as they can, and grow as tall as they possibly can!"

All of us—young or old—have seeds of greatness inside us. It takes a lifetime for those seeds to germinate, sprout, grow and bear great fruits like success, wealth, happiness, and fulfillment. To reach our full potential and bear many fruits, we have to keep growing. And that's what we can expect from our children as well.

So, one early morning on our way to school, I told Jason and Matthew that I had exciting news to announce that night.

"What is it, Mom?" Jason asked.

"Just wait until tonight," I responded with a big warm smile. "I bet you're gonna like it."

They must have thought about it all day. After school and basketball practice, as soon as we were all around the dinner table, Matthew asked, "So, Mom, what is the big announcement you talked about this morning?"

"Oh, I created a brand new project for you!" I shouted gleefully.

Dead silence. They looked at me nervously—what more could Mom possibly do? "But wait a minute," I said, "Let me grab my camera first!" I ran to get the camera.

Why bring a camera into the middle of this awkward moment?

A long time ago I started the LEE FAMILY movie, and I constantly add to it. "My favorite movie is the LEE FAMILY movie," I often said. "I love all of our moments together—good and bad—because at the end of it all, they are what make our life beautiful."

Now the LEE FAMILY movie brunch is a holiday tradition. Every Thanksgiving morning we eat a late breakfast and watch our family videos, from the boys' birth up to the most recent years. It's hilarious! We laugh and cry, remembering how precious our moments together are, and how thankful we are for each one.

So, as I announced the new project, I took pictures to capture those unforgettable moments—the disbelief, the confusion, and finally, the excitement.

The Journey to Greatness Project

That night I introduced the Journey to Greatness Project—a more enhanced and intensified challenge designed to help my boys become more holistic people, and more balanced leaders in their journey of life. I set higher expectations for them by creating something outside their comfort zone and different from their normal way of thinking.

Of course, changes are rarely easy to accept at first. That night we had a long conversation. But by the end of the two-hour meeting, they were pumped up and ready to go.

Does that sound too good to be true? Here's why they got excited:

The Journey to Greatness Project included an upgraded Morning Stuff Allowance, renamed "Super Morning Stuff Allowance." It included the normal things the boys were already comfortable with, plus several new incentives with which to earn more rewards and recognition.

For the meeting, I had prepared the chart below and given it to each of them before beginning my exciting presentation. (Can you tell I'm used to giving presentations to my business clients? I did the same for my boys, but in a way that was appropriate to their age.) This chart can be downloaded from the website www.nomoneymonster.com.

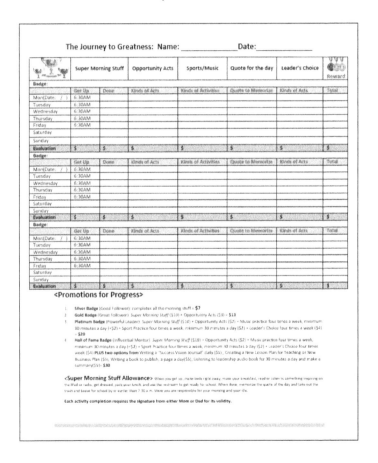

The Journey to Greatness Project has six different key categories:

1. Four Badge System
2. Super Morning Stuff
3. Opportunity Acts
4. Sports/Music/Language
5. Quote for the day
6. Leader's Choice

It might sound a little overwhelming—even to you, the adult reader—but when I broke it down and presented it to them one thing at a time, it was easy enough for them to understand. That's how you eat an elephant right? One bite at a time!

The Four Badge System

The first essential component was the "Four Badge System." You can see the details under "Promotions for Progress" at the bottom of the chart. "This badge system plays a very important role in the Journey to Greatness Project," I told them.

When I said "the badge system," their eyes got bigger because they knew about Boy Scout badges. Boy Scouts of America (BSA) and Girl Scouts of America (GSA) have a fabulous merit badge system that consists of more than 130 merit badges. Any member can earn a badge at any time. All they need to do is to pick one and complete the tasks that are part of it to get a badge at the end. I am not a Boy Scout mom, but I'm fascinated by the Boy Scouts and Girl Scouts who set higher goals—and set themselves apart from most kids—by working to acquire the badges. Nobody can do everything, but everybody can do *something!*

My boys were already interested in earning badges because they knew the story of Russell, the young Boy Scout in the Disney movie *Up* who went through a lot of difficulties to help Mr. Frederickson, an old and lonely man. At the end of their adventure together, Russell was rewarded with a badge and a lot of recognition. That's the same spirit of the Boy Scouts I just mentioned! Jason and Matthew wanted to be like Russell because he was a cool kid—he did something to help another person, and earned a cool badge as a reward.

In my Journey to Greatness system I have four different badges—beginning with Silver and progressing to Gold, and Platinum, until finally you reach the Hall of Fame.

Both my boys love playing sports, so the Hall of Fame badge instantly got their attention. The Hall of Fame—the place where all athletes aspire to be. And here, my boys had a chance to be in a version of one—I could see their imaginations running wild as they pictured themselves getting there!

"What do these badges mean, Mom? How can we move up?" Matthew asked. They'd just come from basketball practice and were very tired—Jason leaned on his dad's shoulder for comfort and Matthew slumped in his chair. But even though they were tired, their minds were alert.

"The Silver badge is for a *Good Follower*," I said. "If you get up on time and do all the things in the morning with a good attitude, you are a good follower. Your reward will be seven dollars a week."

They seemed a little confused by all these new ideas, but they looked at me with a concentrated, wide-eyed gaze that showed me they were still interested.

"But you want to get a Gold badge or above, because a Gold badge is for a *Great Follower*. A Great Follower is a person who does more than just follow the rules. If you do the Super Morning Stuff instead of just regular Morning Stuff, and you complete Opportunity Acts from Monday through Friday, you are a Great Follower. You will get a total of thirteen dollars—ten dollars for Super Morning Stuff *plus* three dollars for Opportunity Acts.

"Mom! Wait a minute!" Matthew cried, throwing up his hands in frustration. "What are all these Super Morning Stuff and Opportunity Acts?" His face told me that he was a little annoyed by the new rules and unfamiliar words.

"Okay, let me explain," I said. "Super Morning Stuff is the same Morning Stuff you've been doing all these years, PLUS just a couple more things!"

"Like what?" Jason asked, his forehead puckering into a worried frown.

"Like, you prepare your own breakfast instead of Mom doing it for you. And while you eat, you read or listen to something inspiring for the day. After that, you memorize the quote for the day, and get your backpack ready for school before 7:30 a.m. That's all!"

(Actually I first came up with "Goals for the day" and tried it for the first week, but shortly after that, I changed it to "Quote for the day.")

"That's all? And we get ten dollars a week instead of seven?" Jason asked, relieved there was nothing super crazy added to what they'd already been doing.

"Yes!" I answered. "And when you do Opportunity Acts five times a week, you get another three dollars on top of that!" But then I realized that I had to clarify what "Opportunity Acts" meant.

"Opportunity Acts are chores. However, chores can sound like a burden sometimes, and some people feel they don't have a choice. Words are powerful, so I decided to change the word *chores* to *opportunity acts*. Because when you help us, you actually create an opportunity to bring value to this family, and we reward those who bring value that makes our lives better."

When they heard "bring value," they immediately associated it with the words of Jim Rohn, the late motivational speaker: "We get paid for bringing value to the marketplace."[2]

I told them this new project was purely based on their free will, and therefore it was just an opportunity, not a requirement. "Nobody will twist your arm," I said. "If you do these things, there is a reward; if you don't—no reward. It's as simple as that."

They were still interested, so it was time to kick it up a notch by introducing the two higher badges.

"Gold is good, but Platinum is better. The Platinum badge is for a *Powerful Leader* who shows a great sense of responsibility and leadership throughout the day. To reach this Platinum level, you do your Super Morning Stuff and Opportunity Acts from Monday through Friday. And you do music or language and sports practice as well as Leader's Choice." The "Leader's Choice" is a more challenging activity they do on their own to help others; the activities can be as simple as cleaning up the house or washing the car, and as involved as cooking a meal for the family or giving massages to their parents and so forth. I showed them on the chart how many times they were required to do those activities to earn the extra points necessary to get the Platinum badge.

What was the reward for the Platinum badge? A whopping *twenty* dollars—ten dollars for the base reward and ten

---

2 https://www.facebook.com/OfficialJimRohn/posts/ 10152783903875635

dollars for extra work. When their faces suddenly lit up, I wasn't surprised. When we earn rewards, our brain releases dopamine, a pleasure hormone that makes us happy. Just the thought of earning that big money and being at Platinum level released dopamine in my sons' brains, as though they already had that cash in their pockets!

Even though I hadn't even explained the Hall of Fame badge yet, their attitudes changed dramatically. Suddenly, they wanted to serve others—Matthew brought me some water and Jason started giving his dad a shoulder massage, asking "Mom, am I doing well? Does this count?" The power of rewards!

I laughed and said, "Not yet. There is one more badge that you need to know about—the ultimate, *the* one-and-only, Hall of Fame badge!"

"The Hall of Fame badge is for an *Influential Mentor* who not only knows how to lead himself, but also knows how to lead, inspire, and help others. For this high position, the *Influential Mentor* must complete all that is required by the Platinum badge, PLUS two more things."

What were the two more things? (Actually there are more than two things, but they can choose two activities out of the total list). The list looks something like: Write a "Success Vision" Journal, work on publishing a book—one page at a time, read something inspiring or listen to a leadership audio book for thirty minutes and write up a summary, create either a new lesson plan to teach other young students in my office or a new business venture plan for their future. These activities should be done four times a week (it's not a daily requirement). And the reward for each of these two extra activities? Five dollars, bringing the total reward for the Hall of Fame badge to a jaw-dropping, eye-popping *thirty* dollars a week—ten dollars for the base reward and twenty dollars for the extra works!

"THIRTY dollars a week? They will have more money than I will at the end of the month!" exclaimed Thomas enviously. I laughed and said, "More than me, too." Now I'd given them the chance—the opportunity—to each make more than a one hundred dollar allowance a month. I knew I was really pushing higher, but I wanted to test my children to see how far they wanted to go.

"Mom, why do we have to do a diary, among so many *other* things?" Matthew asked. He was a little frustrated.

"It's not just a diary," I said. "I am talking about a journal. The difference between a diary and a journal is that in a diary, you write personal things like what happens at school each day and how you feel about it, and things like that. But in a journal, you record something meaningful that you learn from the books you read, or from audio books we listen to, or from other people you've talked to—something that moves you forward."

"I don't know about a journal, Mom … I don't think I can do it," Jason said.

I patted him gently on the shoulder and said, "Don't worry, Jason. Nobody will ask you to do it. It is only you who will demand that of yourself."

As our two-hour conversation was coming to an end, I concluded my presentation. "The decision is yours, boys. It's totally up to you whether or not you want to reach higher. This project will start next Monday morning!"

"What badge are we in right now, Mom?" asked Jason, "Are we Gold now?"

"Nope! Since it's a new program, you start from Silver, and you can move up from there." At first, they looked at me in disbelief that they'd have to start all over from the very bottom, but then they brightened up at the thought of all that money.

That was the end of our family discussion that night, but it was just the beginning. I could feel that something inside them was already moving toward the goals they'd set deep in their minds, and it was exciting to *me*. I could hardly wait for the next Monday!

At this point, some parents might say, "It's like a military boot camp. It's too hard for my children! It's impossible with my kids!"

My answer to that is, first, what's wrong with being like a military boot camp? Isn't life a training ground? Don't we learn as we grow and grow as we learn?

Some parents are afraid of the idea of having their children work hard; they treat their children like delicate flowers in the greenhouse, or even worse, put them on a pedestal and almost worship them. No wonder those children never grow up to be the men and women they were created to be—they never learn how to.

And second, why is it "impossible with my kids?" When you spell 'impossible,' doesn't it sound like, "I am possible?" If you see it as impossible, that's how your kids will see it. See it in a more affirming way, and your kids will follow your lead. Remember Chapter One, in which we talked about how the parent's attitude influences their child?

The National Association of Secondary School Principals (NASSP)[3] says that setting high behavior expectations in the classroom results in greater academic success. For our children, high academic success means better networking among those who can further their careers and their lives. This level of academic success at every age also means that our children gain confidence, social skills, and personal fortitude. It also means they learn to expect more from their world. Why should we expect less from our children than life will expect of them?

The best gift we can give to our children is time—the time we spend with them. Not only time spent at the

---

3 http://www.nassp.org/tabid/3788/default.aspx?topic=Expectations_
Do_You_Have_Them_Do_Students_Get_Them

playground, music institute, dance class, or shopping mall, but time well-spent to *EQUIP THEM AND PREPARE THEM FOR THEIR FUTURE IN EVERY POSSIBLE WAY.* Inevitably, the area of finance will determine an important part of their future.

The time you take to make charts, create incentives, talk about goals, or teach new concepts about money is time invested in your child's financial future. Taking the time to give your child a reward like a trip to the movies or a special event gives you both another memory and puts another brick of stability in the foundation of their confidence.

As parents, we are not only influential to their world, we are THE most powerful influence in their world.

A Couple of Suggestions

I understand that this Journey to Greatness Project is a lot more challenging than the Morning Stuff Allowance Project or the Special Incentive Project. Some of you with very young children may want to stay with the Morning Stuff Allowance Project we discussed in Habit 3 until your children can really handle it with no problems. Then test the waters later. If that's you, you can skip this chapter until the right time comes.

Here are our Super Morning Stuff requirements. Every family has different needs, and your list will reflect what's important to you.

Super Morning Stuff Allowance

1. When you get up, make your beds right away
2. Get dressed and use the restroom
3. Prepare your breakfast
4. While eating, read or listen to something inspiring
5. Get your backpack ready for school
6. Memorize the inspiring quote for the day
7. Leave for school before 7:30 a.m.
8. Show that you are responsible for your morning and your life

Each day's activity completion requires a signature from either Mom or Dad.

But those of you who have already implemented the Morning Stuff Allowance Project and Special Incentive Project and have seen success in your children's day-to-day lives can try this project now.

The amounts I gave my sons fit with our family income. If you feel that you can't take on the Journey to Greatness Project because of the financial demand it requires from your budget, adjust accordingly. The goal is to reward your child for increased and sustained effort, not break the family bank!

In a nutshell, here is a brief description of what the Four Badge System is all about. You can tone it down a little or alter it so it better suits your children's needs and their targeted goals.

Four Badge System

1. **Silver Badge/Good Follower:**
   • Successfully completes all the Morning Stuff = **$7**

2. **Gold Badge/Great Follower:**
   • Super Morning Stuff ($10)
   • Opportunity Acts ($3) = **$13**

3. **Platinum Badge/Powerful Leader:**
   • Super Morning Stuff ($10)
   • Opportunity Acts ($3)
   • Music Practice or Language 4x/week, minimum
     30 minutes ($2)
   • Sport Practice 4x/week, minimum 30 minutes ($2)
   • Leader's Choice 4x/week ($3) **Total = $20**

4. **Hall of Fame Badge/Influential Mentor:**
   • Super Morning Stuff ($10)
   • Opportunity Acts ($3)
   • Music Practice or Language 4x/week, minimum
     30 minutes ($2)
   • Sport Practice 4x/week, minimum 30 minutes ($2)
   • Leader's Choice 4x/week ($3)

(Choose Two More Options Below)
   • Writing a Success Vision Journal 4x/week (Make a
     summary) ($5)
   • Writing a book to publish 4x/week, minimum one
     page ($5)
   • Writing a lesson plan for teaching or business plan
     4x/week ($5)
   • Watching inspiring videos and make a summary
     4x/week, minimum 30 minutes ($5) **Total = $30**

The Journey to Greatness chart can be downloaded from this website: www.nomoneymonster.com.

Some people might think, *What a lot of work to do! Let the kids just be kids. Let them play!*

Well, I agree, *partially*. Even the famous proverb says, "All work and no play makes Jack a dull boy." Jack needs a balanced life to keep him from having a dull life. The right balance between school studies, chores, play, and creative activities is something you create for your children until they are old enough to create their own.

Childhood is not only about growing a body, but also about growing a mentality. Children thrive when given high (but appropriate) expectations, and will strive to achieve those higher goals.

You can see that for my sons, those expectations took many forms. Your lifestyle and your child may have different components, but the goal is still the same—reach higher, like the growing tree!

Let's go back to the Book Project as an example. Do you think it was a lot to ask of six-year-olds who also went to school and played sports and engaged in so many other things? It wasn't. It was a lot to ask, but in a very fair way, with age-appropriate goals. My sons weren't miserable; they simply rose to the challenge set before them.

If I had said to them that they only needed to read one book per week, that's what they would have done. But when I said they needed to do *three*, that's what they managed to do. And they didn't just read three books, they wrote book reports about them.

Because I set high goals for them to reach, they strove to do it. What they got in return was money, their parents' approval, their teachers' acknowledgment of their accomplishments, a reward from the local library, and recognition from their peers.

But more important, my sons gained pride, self-confidence, time-management skills, better writing skills, reading enjoyment, ease in their schoolwork, and the knowledge that they can set and meet goals.

Dr. Maxwell Maltz, author of the classic *Psycho-Cybernetics*, said that human beings have a built-in, goal-seeking "success mechanism" that is part of the subconscious mind—similar to a precision guided missile that continually makes adjustments and corrections in order to hit its target.

Wow! What amazing beings we all are!

It's exciting to know that we have that built-in success mechanism, and so do our young children. As parents, all we need to do is give our children a target to aim at. Set higher goals and expectations, and this success mechanism will find answers to problems and work its own miracles.

Now, let's go back to our Journey to Greatness Project. To all the moms and dads out there wondering how my boys did the first week, I am here to tell you that they did it. Both boys advanced from the Silver badge to the Gold badge after *just* the first week!

Here's what they did: As soon as the alarm clock rang, they jumped up and made their beds, came to the kitchen, and prepared their own breakfast (a bowl of cereal with milk). And they searched for something inspiring to listen to while eating. The very first day, they watched educational math or science videos on my iPad; on other days I tuned into Joel Osteen, Jim Rohn, Les Brown, Tony Robbins, or Jack Canfield, and they listened together.

After that, they packed their school bags, got ready for school, took out the trash, or watered the plants for their Opportunity Acts for that day. They each memorized their quote for the day, and left for school before 7:30 a.m.

The first week inspiring quotes they memorized are:

- Always do your best. What you plant now you will harvest later.

- Dream no small dreams for they have no power to move the hearts of men.

- Be the change that you wish to see in the world.

- Expect problems and eat them for breakfast.

- Start by doing what's necessary; then do what's possible; and suddenly you are doing the impossible.

This is still an ongoing project. I usually ask them to read their quote out loud in the morning right before they leave for school. They have all day to work on remembering it, and then, after dinner, I ask them to repeat it until they say it with 100 percent accuracy. To have your own chart to fill out, turn to the back of the book. It can be also downloaded from the website: www.nomoneymonster.com

During the first several months, they have memorized more than 100 quotes through repetition.

*The First Journey to Greatness Project Chart with
Daily Activity note. Soon after the first week, I changed
"Goals for the Day" to "Quote for the Day."*

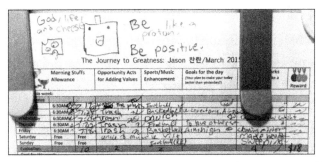

*Matthew's First-week Journey to Greatness Chart. He had a flu at
that time, so most of the days, his goal for the day was healing.*

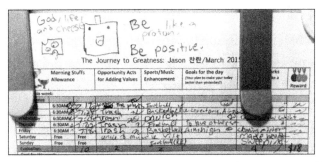

*Jason's First-week Journey to Greatness Chart. I especially
liked "to love others" as his goal for the day.*

As their Journey to Greatness Project continued, they came back from school, practiced sports, and found ways to do more "Leader's Choice" work. They cleaned my car windows at the gas station, cleaned all the mirrors and glass furniture at home, and mopped and swept all the floors in the house. Jason even got up early that Saturday morning to make scrambled eggs for the family. On a couple of days, I saw them taking notes while they listened to a recommendation of their daddy's, Brian Tracy's *10 Keys to Personal Power* on Youtube. Are they planning to reach the Hall of Fame? That remains to be seen!

The big difference I noticed was that they seemed to be clearer about what they were doing and why they were doing it, and most important, they understood the leadership they'd shown by voluntarily taking on acts of service for the good of others. They found that they enjoyed helping and serving others.

Of course, they also wanted the great reward, but it was bigger than just wanting rewards. They seemed to really get it, the meaning of how to live a life that's better each day through clear, purpose-driven actions.

The Wednesday after I rolled out this new project, they attended their church youth group meeting. There they had a discussion about the topic of walking on a Wide Road or a Narrow Road, and how it is linked to our day-to-day lives.

Jason said, "It's like our alarm clock. The alarm clock has a big, wide snooze button, and a small, narrow on/off button. So when the alarm clock rings, many people just press the snooze button until finally they're ready to get up. By doing that, they waste a lot of time. In the same way, when we have important things to do, many people like to snooze ... snooze ... snooze ... until later. By the time they are ready, they have already wasted a lot of time and opportunities, and missed out on many great things in life."

I want to say "Amen!" to that, and I hope that they learned this concept from my many projects. But whatever the source is, the important thing is that it's working. They are growing wiser, and they are becoming masters of their lives.

Life will ask a lot of our children, and they will choose whether they want to walk on wide roads or narrow roads, as the Bible describes. But if they learn at this early age that they are capable of reaching goals and making good decisions, they will set those same standards for themselves as adults in the workforce, in their own financial designs, and in the ways they lead others.

THE TAKEAWAY

Set high goals for your children that they can reach, if they work at it. The higher the goal, the bigger the reward they earn.

Chapter Five

Habit #5:
Learn Personal
Finance By Playing

"Necessity is the mother of invention," says an old English proverb, and in the spirit of this proverb, I created many different projects for my sons whenever the need arose.

When they were in third grade, I came up with a plan to prepare my boys for the real world of personal finance that they would explore as young adults. And before that time arrived, I wanted them to experience a glimpse of what it would be like to get a part-time job, work for an employer, run their own business, manage their customers, and live a successful life.

I believed my eight-year-old sons were old enough to handle the pressure of finding a job, making money, paying the bills, making their customers happy, and running a profitable business—if they could do it in a safe environment at home, under their mommy's supervision!

I wanted to give them a training playground where they could try different things related to finance—go through trials and errors, stumble and fall, make mistakes, and get back up (without necessarily losing real money!). I wanted them to feel the stress but learn how to manage it, and to learn how to make better choices for a better future.

That need inspired me to create another new project called the "Finance Book Project." Yep! It was another book project for my boys!

The Finance Book Project

Jason and Matthew were already busy doing many things: school-related projects, homework, basketball practice, Taekwondo class, swimming class, and church activities—and on top of all that were the daily Morning Stuff Allowance and Special Incentive Project. I was well aware that every day there was something going on in their schedule, but this new project was as important as whatever they were doing at that time, if not more important.

As usual, on the night of my new project launch, I had a family discussion at our dinner table where I introduced the Finance Book Project and explained how it worked.

"The purpose of this project is big," I said to my boys, "and it's much bigger than who you are. It's about learning personal finance." The boys seemed half excited and half worried. Every time I rolled out a new project, they were a little nervous at first. But when they found that it wasn't as crazy as they'd thought, they relaxed.

Your kids will probably do the same thing. They might be nervous or even resistant to a new project or idea. But if the idea is presented in a positive way—so that they see enough benefits to be inspired—they can surprise themselves (and you).

"This is a big project," I told them, "and therefore the reward is big, too!"

"How big, Mom?" they both asked simultaneously.

"As much as THREE HUNDRED dollars!" I shouted, pointing to the window, "Only the sky is the limit!" Jason and Matthew just stared at me, mouths open.

"This is how it is going to work: When you write a full page per topic, each page counts as ten points, and ten points equals ten dollars."

"Writing about what, Mom?" Jason asked.

"Things about money! You are going to write essays, and I will put them all together later to make a book! Isn't it cool? When you write ten pages, you get a hundred points, and therefore a hundred dollars—and if you write thirty pages, you get three hundred points, equaling three hundred dollars. You will receive a reward when the book gets published."

At first, they were silent, unable to believe these big numbers. I understood this non-verbal language and didn't try to convince them to like the project right away.

"I will e-mail you two topics a week. You can finish them anytime you want before Saturday, and e-mail them back to me whenever your work is ready. At the end of each weekend, I'll review your essays and credit their total points according to their level of excellence. It's as simple as that. Have fun, boys! You will love it!" Thomas was very supportive of this idea and encouraged them to do their best.

As a mom and a writer myself, I was excited about this new project because it would give me an opportunity to get a sneak peek at what was going on in my children's minds—the mysterious world of the unknown.

When we set goals for our children that push them to achieve outside their comfort zones, it's important to acknowledge that they're being challenged. But it's also important for us, as parents, to convey confidence that they can do it. Presenting challenges with enthusiasm excites your child's brain and encourages them to expect their own success, even if it means extra work.

A note about money that bears repeating: The goal here is to increase the reward according to the effort your child has to make, and according to your ability to *consistently* deliver what you promise. Three hundred dollars is a huge amount of money for a third grader, and even for many parents in their third decade of life. As I write this book, my boys are eleven years old, and the book hasn't come out yet. When it's published, later this year or next year, they will get their promised reward! Your personal finance project for your children can be different from ours, so be creative and tailor this system of increasing responsibilities and performance to your family's values and budget.

Moving to a Three-Dimensional World Experience

Some of you might wonder how this Finance Book Project is different from the Amazing Book Project. The Amazing Book Project involves reading books and writing reports about them. During the process, your children choose any book they want to read.

But the Finance Book Project is focused on reading and writing about *personal finance,* using various resources available on the Internet—interactive games, finance-related videos, articles, and even biographies of financially successful people.

When your child is successful with the Morning Stuff Allowance and the Special Incentive Project, implementing the Finance Book Project is a great way to add a new goal to help them learn to enjoy reading and writing about finance.

However, you have to be careful that your children aren't just mindlessly going through the routine of reading books and writing about them. That unthinking way of writing is like a two-dimensional world where they can draw circular balls of many different colors and sizes. They look great on paper, and they're fun to draw and color, but kids can't play with them because they aren't three-dimensional.

If they just read and write, but don't investigate or analyze, their understanding is superficial. For them to go beyond the mere length and width of two-dimensional learning requires your parental input. The two-dimensional world is great, but the three-dimensional world is better! We all love 3-D, and the Finance Book Project is like a 3-D world of reading and writing that builds on the skills your child developed through the previous book project.

As a mom who is fortunate to be in the world of personal finance, my desire was to create a safe, supervised finance playground in 3-D where my sons could play, explore, and learn lots of new things on their own. In the 3-D world, our children don't just draw the two-dimensional ball; they pick it up and play with it, thereby adding the third-dimension—depth. In terms of learning about the real world, depth incorporates layered demands like time management, supply sourcing, and profit margins.

And as you'll see in this chapter, the Internet offers many enjoyable ways to learn these complex ideas. With the tools I discuss, you can create a playground filled with hidden treasures for your children.

"In this playground," I said, "there is only one simple rule to keep, and that is to read Mommy's e-mail instructions every week and to do your best."

When they were in the first grade, I created their e-mail accounts and used these to occasionally send encouraging messages, and now the time had come for them to get their hands dirty. When I sent my first e-mail to Jason and Matthew about the Finance Book Project, I wanted to know what they were thinking about money, so I asked these two questions:

1. What is money?
2. Why is it important to save money for the future?

A couple of days later, Jason responded, "Money is the thing you use to buy things and to live a great life. It is very important to save money for your retirement so that you can retire with enough money to live with."

Retirement? I thought it was brilliant that he was thinking about retirement at such a young age.

He continued, "With the money in my savings, I would go to my bank. With my spending money, I would buy gifts for my parents and family. For example, I would get this makeup smell thingy called cologne for my dad as a present."

I recalled how, for Christmas the year before, Jason and Matthew had saved enough money to buy their dad a cologne called "Clutch." Every time Thomas put on his new cologne, they shouted, "It smells really good, Daddy!"

Giving to others is its own reward, which we'll cover in Habit 7. My point with this story is to show the satisfaction your children can derive from knowing they are powerful and can affect others.

"I think that by the time I am ready to go to college, I would have saved $100,000. My mom made me a wallet where my money goes in. I got a frog bank, but I traded my frog bank for Matthew's panda bank."

I laughed, but also saw the fruits of my labors. I felt like a golden sun was shining down on me—Jason was definitely on the right track toward his goal.

What about Matthew?

"Well, I will tell you my version of money," Matthew said. "You see, money is used to buy things in your daily life. Duh!"

He went on: "My parents give me allowance every week, and where does that money go to? My bank account! I get allowance when I do chores and stuff, including brushing my teeth! Yuck! Anyway, half of the money I receive goes to my savings account, and the other half goes to my spending account. The money in my spending account is used to buy gifts and stuff. And for my mom's birthday and last Christmas, I bought her two bracelets."

Yep, he did. He saved enough money to buy me nice bracelets from two of my favorite stores. It feels like yesterday that he proudly paid for my gifts with his own money.

"The money I save is used for college, but what happens if I can't make it to college? Well, everybody has to pass the first grade! That is why the first grade tables are so small—so they won't fit as an adult! But if I get a scholarship, then what will the money be used for? It would be used for my family, food, or I can donate it to a country that is less fortunate than I. So, I should save everything that I get because a penny saved is a penny earned."

I was relieved to know that his thinking about money was not only healthy, but somewhat profound. He reinforced the idea that how we talk about money is how our children learn to think about it.

That night, I shared my feedback with my boys and wrote down their points for those essays. The positive feedback gave them the momentum to keep going.

These stories are cute, but telling. They show us that every child sees the world in a unique way. That means every child will learn in his or her own unique way, and what works for one may not work the same way for another. With all the projects in this book, you can decide which appeals to your child's personality and abilities. Tailor them to reflect your family's values, desires, and budget.

Ask the questions that will make your children *think*. They will tell you the most marvelous things! It can make you wonder where the ideas are from and where they learned what they know.

1. What is money? Why is it important to save money?
2. How can you make money in this marketplace?
3. If you don't get an allowance from your parents, where can you go to earn money?
4. What would you like to do if you had a million dollars right now?
5. What does college mean to you? How will you save money for college?

I asked the same questions of my boys. Here's a snippet from Jason's response :

"The way you can make money in this marketplace is by getting a job or doing the chores, which is what I do. The chores that I do usually are taking out the trash, sweeping the leaves, watering the plants, and sometimes trimming the leaves of the bushes so that they won't grow too long. Then, if I do my chores five times a week and finish getting ready [for school] by

7:30, I will get seven dollars per week. In order to get seven dollars, I would also have to show good leadership like doing my work without anyone telling me or making my report the best it could be or making all the ... bed covers with excellence.

"However, if I don't get money from my parents, things that I can do to earn money from others are like washing the car, sweeping the dusty floor, taking the groceries inside the house, trim the weeds or the dead leaves, green up the garden by planting new plants, or preparing food for a fellow friend. My neighbor, Ms. Kelly, might be willing to give me allowance. I don't want to stop having allowance, but if that is my only choice, I would do the chores for others to get allowance.

"Money to me is the way of life. If you don't have money, you can't buy anything. Then, your financial plan would be ruined and you wouldn't have enough money to take care of yourself later. The meaning of money for me is like the key to living a successful life. If you have a lot of money now, you should save it, not spend it all. Some people say spend spend spend. No! You should save even though you don't get an item you want right now. You would be happy when you retire because then you would already have enough money in your savings. We save our money at [the bank], and we move our money to [the financial company], where we make more investments. When I retire, I will have lots of precious money.

"If I had a million dollars, I would spend a portion of it on a big family trip to Paris, Italy, Hawaii, Egypt, and South Korea. I would rent a hotel there and invite some of my family members and enjoy [it]. The rest of my money would be put in a place, where I can save my money and make investment for other trips so that my family can have many great experiences."

In his essay about college, Matthew was very specific about numbers related to it:

"College is a chance to be in the middle class in the United States of America, but it is a very expensive and sacrificing ticket. And its cost grows higher every year, so you should start saving. The annual cost for a college education is about $7,000 for a community college and about $35,000 for a private college. Those are a lot of numbers, but if you save at an early start, then it won't be as bad as it seems.

"Honestly, I feel a little bit scared about going to college. I mean like how will you get so much money and will it be enough? There is just so many things I am worried about. Don't panic bro. If you can save at an early age and move your money to a stock market, I am sure you can get enough money for college, but try to work hard so you can have a shot about having a free college.

"If you ask me, I think Princeton University is the best college, but it is very expensive. It is about $56,750 for the year of 2013–2014, but remember, it will keep growing. It is important to go to college because it teaches you more than what they teach you in high school. If you are going to get a job and if you show the owner your college master's degree, there is a better chance that he is going to give you a very important place in the company because you are trustable."

How did an eight-year-old learn all about the costs and expenses of college? I sent him a website link to do some research for his essay. And where did this idea of going to Princeton come from? Ever since they were two or three, I'd been telling them that Princeton is one of the best schools in the world.

Princeton is a great school, but who can foresee the future? Neither of my sons may decide to go to Princeton when they grow up, or the school may not accept them as students. But it's okay because, as the late W. Clement Stone said, "You aim for the moon. If you miss, you may hit a star."

Jason and Matthew familiarized themselves with many finance-related websites I sent to them for their project, and each one of them taught something new to my boys. Check out this list of websites that I personally found useful for my kids. (Note: these websites were used at the time of writing and publishing this book, but may have had updates since.) You can use them to give your children a fun education that will help them for the rest of their lives:

1. **Federal Reserve Bank of Cleveland**
   Website: www.clevelandfed.org

This is a great website—very interesting and educational. Click 'Learning Center' and then go to 'Money Museum' on the top menu and explore! Most of the information here is practical and useful, and it's also fun to learn things from interactive online games. My boys especially liked the game *Escape from Barter Islands,* which is a fun game that prompts thinking on the role of money in an economy, through barter and trade, as it says.

Also try these other great games on this website:

- *Money Word Search*
- *Great Minds Think: A Kid's Guide to Money*
- *Explore Money from Around the World*

2. **Kids Math Games**
   Website: www.kidsmathgamesonline.com

I am so glad I didn't overlook this website, although I was very tempted to. It's not a personal finance website, but a math website. It teaches mathematics from addition to multiplication and has a wide range of free math games, interactive learning activities, and fun math resources.

But it wasn't until I decided to stay and explore some of the pages that I became more interested in this website, which features a number of exciting, money-related games for kids, like *Coffee Shop* and *Lemonade Stand*. Click 'Money' on the dropdown menu. Through these interactive games, my boys had the great experience of running their own businesses and created unforgettable memories. I'd like to share some of their experiences.

Coffee Shop

My boys first tried the *Lemonade Stand* game, which was as easy as a breeze in the air. But when they tackled the higher-level *Coffee Shop* game, I noticed that they both struggled—big time. They didn't seem to understand how to make good coffee, how to make their customers happy, and how to make profits out of this business. They tried this game over and over, but kept failing.

At first, Jason worked alone, but he didn't have the success he wanted. He wrote about first business adventure experience:

"I started a coffee shop called the Coffee Mug, and it wasn't easy to run the business. I had to lower the price when the people drank on a hot day (about $2.59) and I would make the price higher when it [was] a cold day ($3.56) because then, people are more desperate to get coffee. I had to keep the prices pretty low because I figured out if my prices are low, I would get more customers and if I get more customers,

I would eventually get a lot more money than only one person buying a cup of coffee that is $5.00. I had to buy a reasonable amount of cups, sugar, coffee, and milk. I had to get about 50 cups, 20 teaspoons of coffee, 20 teaspoons of sugar, and 40 servings of milk."

Later, Thomas and I both came onboard to help them individually, but that didn't seem to work, either. Parents don't always have the right answers!

After Matthew worked with Thomas and found the coffee business still wasn't doing well, he shared his frustrating yet memorable experiences in his essay:

"On June 8, 2013, my daddy and I played a coffee shop game. We started off with 30 dollars. The point of the game was to make as much money as I could in 14 days. We spent too much money on cups, and our milk was always spoiling because we got too much milk. We raised the prices really high when it was cold or freezing (4 dollars) and we [lowered] the prices when it was really warm (1 dollar). Our inventory was running low and people couldn't buy any more coffee. We made about 50 dollars at the end of 14 days. If we got less cups, then we would have got more money at the end and if we didn't get so much milk, then we would have got more money too."

Finally, the boys decided to work together as a team. Let me tell you—that wasn't easy, either! They experienced some success … followed by lots of failures. But in the end, it was all worth their time, because they found love and support from one another and created lots of great memories.

Jason wrote: "Today, I didn't do that well in the coffee game because I kept on losing all my inventory and I kept on getting sold out. There were so many costumers left and if I just had some more milk, sugar, cups, and coffee, I would have gotten a lot more money than only about seven bucks. When I had enough inventory and enough servings for everyone, I got a lot more money than only 4 or 5 dollars. I think I should have saved a lot of money for the cold days so that lots of people would come and buy their coffee and we [Jason and Matthew] won't run out of money. People said the price was perfect, so I should get enough inventory to not get sold out, especially on really cold days."

Matthew: "On June 15, 2013, my brother Jason and I played a coffee shop game together because mom said that we should work as a team. We started off with thirty dollars. We were trying to set a goal of 60 dollars. We got very little cups and very little milk. We had very little inventory, so it was very hard to make money. We tried to get more inventory, but then our coffee was going stale, our milk was spoiling, and ants were invading our sugar. We had too little cups so we had to spend so much money on them. At the end, we only made 11 dollars. I think I should get the middle amount of inventory next time like twenty of everything. Many people liked our price and coffee and we had a good reputation. It was a bummer that it didn't go the way we wanted, but I loved working with my brother."

"... **but I loved working with my brother.**" I read this sentence over and over, and felt so warm inside. You get it ... right?

As a mom, my main concern wasn't about my eight-year-old boys figuring out how to successfully run a coffee shop. It was about them working together as a team and learning from the mistakes they made, as well as appreciating one another for being there during difficult times.

This Coffee Shop game is great, and I highly recommend it to parents with young children, because it really makes them *think*. And because it's fun, they'll try hard to come up with solutions. Last year, Jason and Matthew tried this game again and they both figured out this game so fast that they couldn't believe how it was so difficult back then. This time it was like a piece of cake (this is why I recommend it for younger children).

3. **Kids.gov**
   Website: http://kids.usa.gov

This website is great too, because it has different categories for kids, teens, parents, and teachers. There's a variety of fun vocational videos—from animal keeper to White House chef. Spend some time on this website and really explore. It has a video about how dollar bills are made, which I used for my project, and which my boys found fun and educational.

4. **The Mint.Org**
   Website: www.themint.org

We used this great website a lot. It turned learning about finance into fun! The information is designed for different age groups—kids, teens, parents, and teachers. Under the kids finance section, my boys tested their financial IQs and learned the basic concepts of earning, saving, spending, and giving.

Your children will learn how to use their money for saving, spending, investing, giving, and so much more. If your children are teenagers, there are many sections devoted for teens' financial growth and success, so you should check it out. In my opinion, it's worthwhile navigating through the whole website, click by click, page by page.

Look at what Jason learned from this website: "I learned about millionaires today. Millionaires usually are entrepreneurs, and they are not the poor people who become millionaires by winning the lottery. The chance of winning [the] lottery is 1 in 17 billion, and you have a better chance getting struck by lightning because that chance is 1 in 9 billion."

And Matthew said, "I learned that millionaires are just ordinary people who choose to do better, to be successful and to do the impossible. They usually are hard workers. You don't need a fancy car or a big mansion to be a millionaire. You don't need somebody to do everything for you when you are a millionaire. Millionaires don't act all fancy and buy really expensive things just because they are millionaires. They spend wisely and save efficiently."

At only eight years old, my boys learned many finance-related terms:

- Signing the back of a check is called *endorsing*.
- An *emergency fund* is a savings plan for unexpected expenses.
- There is a disadvantage to using a credit card because you may increase *impulse buying*.
- 401(k) account contributions are made on a pretax basis.
- Common *maturity dates* for certificates of deposit are three, six, or twelve months.
- A *blue-chip stock* is a stock from a large, financially sound company.

How well they understand all these terms is a secondary concern for me; what excites me is that all this information will be stored in their subconscious minds, and it will re-emerge whenever they need it in the future.

5. **Practical Money Skills for life**
   Website: www.practicalmoneyskills.com

I recommend this website to everyone. It's loaded with lots of practical information and tools you can utilize from day one, and it covers many areas of personal finance—from saving, education, and college all the way to retirement. I used pretty much every page here as part of my project.

There are also cool games to develop your children's money management skills and to enhance their basic understanding of finance. Jason and Matthew liked the fast-paced, interactive sports games like football and soccer. Check out this list of excellent games:

- Cash Puzzler
- Financial Football
- Financial Soccer
- Money Metropolis
- Road Trip to Savings
- Peter Pig's Money Counter
- Countdown to Retirement

When Matthew played Money Metropolis, he said that he learned how to save money more effectively by choosing the right kind of job. He wrote, "I chose raking. At first it took a lot of time to rake all the leaves into one pile. I received ten dollars every time I finished, and I was soon able to get a leaf blower. It made me money so much easier than raking. I could make twice the amount of money with the same time. There were some other jobs too. There were lawn mowing, paper delivering, babysitting and working in a gas station. The reason why I didn't choose these jobs was because they didn't give me money as easily as a leaf blower. The point is that if you work hard in the beginning, then you can rest later on."

Jason, on the other hand, struggled through all kinds of chores to make money, and later learned from his brother the secret of making more money with less time and less work. He also learned a subtler lesson about using the wisdom of others to enhance his own success. Jason wrote, "Some things I did as chores to get money [were] blowing the leaves, babysitting, and filling gas in people's cars in the gas station. Filling the people's cars was difficult because I had to fill up the 20 cars very quickly. This was very hard, so that is why I only did this once or twice. I did lots of babysitting. It wasn't hard because I had quick hands, but even with my quick hands, it wasn't easy when everything started ringing and I had to turn everything off because the baby would wake up."

And he continued, "Finally, I got the blower. In the beginning, I didn't have enough money for the blower. I heard Matthew say that he got all his money by blowing leaves, and I wanted to do that too. So I saved forty bucks and bought the blower. A reason I bought it was because it was a lot faster than raking with a rake. My efficiency level was getting higher and I could get ten bucks in only 3 seconds. It took 3 minutes raking with the rake, but with the same amount of leaves, I could blow and get the money in only 3 seconds!"

6. **Secret Millionaires Club**
   Website: www.smckids.com

On this website, your kids will actually meet the animated figure of Warren Buffet, one of the wealthiest men alive! In each episode, Warren mentors a group of business-minded kids to solve different financial challenges. My boys watched all twenty-six episodes in a short amount of time. They just couldn't help it, because each episode was so much fun!

7. **US Currency**

Website: www.newmoney.gov

If you want your children to know about US currency in great detail, this is the right place for you! My boys learned a lot about the history of US Currency here—basic things like how the various denominations of dollar bills look, and who is on each bill. On this website, your children will learn that the United States began printing money in 1877, and that 1957 was the first year that "In God We Trust" was printed on paper currency.

Your children may get bored here if you don't make it fun and interactive. To make it interesting, I asked my boys to make a copy of each currency image and write down the name of the person on the image, from $1 to $100,000. Right after that, I gave them a quick quiz to reinforce what they'd just memorized. Here is the list of the dollar bill presidents:

- **$1.00:** George Washington
- **$2.00:** Thomas Jefferson
- **$5.00:** Abraham Lincoln
- **$10.00:** Alexander Hamilton (he was not a president)
- **$20.00:** Andrew Jackson
- **$50.00:** Ulysses S. Grant
- **$100.00:** Benjamin Franklin (he was not a president)

- **$500.00:** William McKinley
- **$1,000:** Grover Cleveland
- **$5,000:** James Madison
- **$10,000:** Salmon P. Chase (he was not a president)
- **$100,000:** Woodrow Wilson

There are many other websites out there that are as useful, educational, and fun as the ones described above, so do your own research. But if you start with the websites above, they will suck you in and lead you to other great sites (and you'll probably want to play the games, too)!

Let's not underestimate the side benefits of these websites. Many parents complain that their child only wants to spend time on the computer. Directing your child's attention to these educational games yields triple rewards—it brings in the computer your child loves to use, educates them (and you!), creates a bond as you work together, and gives you both a positive way to see and interact with finances.

Great Questions to Ask

By now, you've noticed that I use motivational speakers to inspire my boys, even though those speakers are adults. Did Jason and Matthew understand 100 percent of what they were listening to? No—but they understood the big concepts, and we could talk about them. Motivational speakers frequently ask you to envision your future. It's a valuable practice for anyone.

The list below stimulates young imaginations to come up with their own ideas and visions. Who knows? Maybe one of these ideas will be the seed of your child's future business!

1. Make a list of twenty things you want to accomplish in your life.
2. Write down ten chores you can do to earn money.
3. How much do you want to earn this year? Why and how?
4. Why is it important for kids to work hard to earn money instead of asking their parents for it?
5. Imagine yourself in twenty years—where are you, where do you live, what do you do, and who are you with?
6. What are you willing to do NOW to get to where you want to be in the future?
7. Describe ten things that you are most proud of achieving in your life so far.

The list can go on and on! Create your own questions, custom-tailored for your children—with a little imagination, you could even make them funny!

Our common objective as parents is to stimulate our children's minds and encourage them to see that there's more to life beyond the reality of what they see and think in this moment. If you haven't done this kind of fun inquiry with your kids before, you will be astonished to find out how they think; it's like they are in an unlimited possibility zone. It can make you laugh and cry at the same time.

Doing the Personal Finance Project and playing finance related Internet games was the first step my sons took toward real-life application of what they had learned. When we took those finance ideas into the actual world of the Los Angeles Farmer's Market, they got to see what happens when logic and intellect meet the temptations that life constantly offers.

THE TAKEAWAY

Writing essays about personal finance and playing Internet money games makes learning fun and teaches real-life skills. Playing these games with your child is a way to spend fun, educational time together.

Chapter Six
Habit #6:
Go Experience the Real World

Recently I learned how a mother eagle trains her eaglets to fly. To my astonishment, I learned that baby eagles will never learn to fly if they are separated from their parents at birth.

In the article "Eagle Flight,"[1] the pastor Bob Stone says, "If we take an eagle and separate it at birth from its parents, it will just grovel around in the dirt like a chicken." Without parental guidance, the eaglets will scratch around where they land, without any protection. If they don't even try to fly, they will stay in the nest, where they can easily become the prey of some wild beast or freeze to death one cold night.

---

1   www.eagleflight.org

That's where the great mother eagle steps in and kicks their butts! One by one, she pushes the little ones out of the nest, because she knows that her eagles will never fly as long as they stay safely inside. At first, the eaglets will fall down, but the mother eagle catches them right before they hit the ground and puts them back into their safe nest. Then she pushes them back out again, over and over, until they finally learn to fly. In this case, the *push* is the greatest gift that the mother eagle can ever give to her offspring.

In the same way, we also must push our children off the cliff of their comfort zone—their safe nest and the world that they are familiar with—for their own good. Just like eaglets, our children won't try to face anything new—especially anything uncomfortable or challenging—until we give them a non-negotiable *push*, just like a mother eagle. Our children may not understand why they are pushed, but we know why, so we keep pushing.

That's what I had to do a few years back. I needed to give Jason and Matthew a push into the real world of finance, and to make them *suffer* a little when they seemed too comfortable with the idea of just working for financial rewards, saving their earnings, and creating a budget. This was their safe nest, and they had to fly!

So one Saturday morning, I told Jason and Matthew that we would go to the Farmer's Market, where they would put what they had learned about budgeting and spending into practice in the real world. I told them that they could shop for anything they wanted to purchase with their own money, as long as it was within their budget.

"Anything, Mommy?" Matthew repeated, excited.

"Yes. Of course." I nodded, giving them two thumbs up.

Back then we lived near the Farmer's Market, so we went there often to eat, hang out, and have fun as a family. The Farmer's Market has had a unique place in the community for more than a hundred years. There are a lot of vendors selling gourmet products, fresh produce, and culturally diverse food selections. Around the market is a shopping mall full of stores just overflowing with toys, candies, and gift items. There are high-end retailers, upscale restaurants, and a movie theater. At the Farmer's Market, everywhere you look, something entices you—and especially your children—to part with every penny in your pocket.

My boys were familiar with the place, and that made it a perfect venue for their first eaglet flight into real life with their hard-earned money.

That Saturday morning, they both had brought their paper wallets in their pockets. They had dreams of spending their own money at LA's oldest toy store. They felt like they were big boys now! They were proud and excited, but I was a little nervous.

We wove our way through the packed Farmer's Market, through stores filled with handmade chocolate, stickers, and souvenirs, until we finally reached the toy store—their final destination. As we neared the toys, Jason and Matthew got more and more excited. Their tone of voice, their light foot-steps, and their huge smiles signaled something we all have experienced—the thrill of throwing our money away!

Their goal was to buy a toy they had dreamed of, and my goal for the day was to teach my eaglets about budgeting and spending—and to make them feel a little uncomfortable and stirred up.

"Today," I said, "the rule is simple. Be wise about your spending and have fun!"

However, before I released them into that land of tempta-tions, I needed to explain to them that they could not buy things over their budget, and that they would have to pay sales tax.

"What's a sales tax, Mommy?" Jason asked.

"A sales tax is something extra that everyone pays for the sale of certain goods or services. For example, when you buy a toy today, the store will charge you a little extra money, and that is a sales tax. The sales tax will then be given to the government so that the government can use it to build roads, schools, hospitals, bridges, and all sorts of things that we use almost every day."

"How much extra, Mommy?" Matthew asked, "Is this enough?" He showed the dollar bills he had in his wallet.

"Yes. It's enough. The sales tax rate is different, depending on where you live. To be safe, just include 10 percent extra whenever you buy things. So if your toy costs $8, then add 10 percent of that to the cost of your toy. Then the total will be $8.80. Okay?"

I didn't want to confuse them with too much information, so I kept it simple. "Okay, Mom!" they crowed as they began their treasure hunt at the store. There were all kinds of enticing toys for kids: Legos, cars, action figures, power vehicles, blocks, building sets, stuffed animals, dinosaurs, and basketballs. It was paradise!

"Mommy, can I buy this?" they asked me every time they saw something nice.

"Remember that you have your own spending money! You earned it, so use it wisely. Look at the price tag, and if you have enough money *and* can pay the sales tax, then you can buy it." Many times, I cringed inside, but I wanted them to make their own choices. "And always save your receipt so you can keep track of your spending."

Matthew wanted to buy a blue hamster toy that some of his friends at school had. It cost about $11, including sales tax.

He liked it a lot because it felt like a real animal and made a cute hamster sound. Jason was playing with it, too. They had always liked the idea of owning a pet, and were craving a puppy, hamster, or cat. But they had to enjoy animals from a distance because of what I said, "Not until we buy a bigger house." So this cute, furry creature tickled their longing for a pet. It was obvious that they wanted it badly, but they both hesitated. They gazed at it, played the sound over and over, giggled, hummed the chipmunk song, and petted the fur. But in the end, they put the toy back on the shelf. I was impressed that, even though they were attracted to the sound it made, its fur, and the novelty of it, they chose not to buy it.

"Why not buy one? You like it, right?" I asked, wondering about their logic. They both had enough money to buy the toy plus another small item.

"It's too expensive, Mommy," said my sad-looking Matthew, holding a dollar item in one hand and his wallet in the other. "I'm gonna just ask Auntie Nancy or Auntie Amy to buy it for me."

Of course, he had a Plan B! He wanted to use OPM (Other People's Money) for his own enjoyment and satisfaction. There is no doubt that they have the greatest aunties in the world! Nancy and Amy have always been especially generous to their first nephews, and those boys knew it! I had to laugh at Matthew's strategy.

Jason also circled around the store a few times, and showed some interest in a couple of other toys there, but ended up with a small item that cost less than two dollars—nothing fancy. They calculated the sales tax and paid for their purchases, got the receipts, and walked out of the store.

I couldn't believe my two eight-year-old boys were walking out of the toy store without buying a fancy toy! Generally, kids are impulsive buyers. Seeing is wanting. Jason and Matthew were obsessed with items like Ninjago, Legos, ttakji (a traditional Korean game played using folded paper disks), and Pokemon cards. These games were all very popular at the kids' school, and almost everyone they knew had them.

So they asked for them—and received them—from their aunties and uncles, their grandparents, and their parents for their birthdays and Christmases. However, to this day, some of those toys sit on the shelf, still wrapped—a waste of money, natural resources, and someone's hard work. The boys weren't too concerned about how much those items cost.

But at the Farmer's Market, when it was *their* turn to spend *their* own money out of *their* pockets to pay for the toys they wanted, they were suddenly more serious and cautious.

Until we went to the Farmer's Market, my sons just worked to get money to save and feel rich. First it went into the piggy bank and the paper wallet, then into the savings bank and investment accounts. It was thrilling and satisfying, but a little abstract. Now, though, they saw how their weeks of work could have suddenly disappeared into someone else's hands in a blink of eye, never to return. It was a powerful, real-life experience for them. That was the very first of many times they took charge of their money to buy things for themselves … or exercised their willpower to resist temptation.

About a year later, our family went grocery shopping at a Korean market in Los Angeles, and in that particular plaza there was a hat kiosk. While I was getting fruits and vegetables at the grocery store, I saw Jason and Matthew trying out hats at the kiosk. By the time I had finished, Jason was checking himself out in the mirror, admiring the nice cap he was wearing.

"Mom, look!" said Jason, modeling an orange and red, flat-bill cap with his favorite brand logo on the top. "Can I have it?" he asked with a gentle smile.

Beside him, Matthew instantly frowned, pointing at the price tag. "Mom, it's almost thirty bucks with tax!"

"Thirty bucks? It's kinda pricy. But you earned it, so use your money wisely! Did you bring your wallet?" I asked Jason. I wanted him to take charge of his own spending and make his own decision.

He hadn't brought his wallet that day, and he said he would take some time to think about it and decide whether it was a good buy. He gave himself a few days to think about it, but not too long after that, he asked me to drive him back to the store. "Mom, I thought about it, and I really like it. Since it is a good brand, I will probably wear it for a long time, so it's worth spending big bucks."

Did I agree? I didn't say a word about it. It was his choice, and I had to honor that. We went back to the store and he paid for the cap with his own savings. It looked very nice on him, and he felt proud.

On the day Jason got his cap, Matthew wanted it, too. "Can I try it on?" he asked. Jason said no at first, because it was a brand new hat, but then he said yes. And when Matthew put it on, he also wanted to have the chic, flat-bill-style cap with the hip urban vibe.

Jason doesn't mind paying extra, as long as he likes something and the quality is good. But Matthew is more practical when it comes to buying things. He said, "I like it, but I don't want to spend thirty bucks just on a hat. Mom, can we go to an outlet store one of these days?"

"Sure. Not anytime soon, though," I replied. I wanted to calm him down a little, although I could sense his desire to buy his hat RIGHT NOW.

I am proud to say that I am a frugal shopper. Ever since I was young, I derived a lot of satisfaction from looking for a great deal. I like to go to outlet stores and use those stores' discount coupons, and when I'm travelling, I find the best plane fares possible online. Thomas is like that, too, and we often brought our baby boys along in shopping carts while we were shopping in outlet malls, discount stores, and factory stores. When they got older, they pushed the carts around these stores while we looked for great overstocked items, clearance items, or even regular, name-brand items that were on sale. After we were done shopping, I often gave my boys a high-five and said, "Mommy just saved lots of bucks today!"

So when Matthew wanted to save his money on a cap, to him it was not a question of "Can I afford it?" but a question of "How can I get the best deal?"

He was willing to wait, so I let him wait a few more days and then took him to several local outlet stores nearby. He looked all over the place for what he wanted and finally found a similar cap with the same brand name. It was a green, flat-bill cap with the logo on the black top. And he saved almost 65 percent in comparison to what Jason had paid for his cap.

"Mom, I just saved lots of bucks today! Isn't this a great deal?" asked Matthew as he walked out the store with a big winner's smile and a stylish hat on his head.

"You got it!" I responded, giving him a loving pat on the forehead.

Jason tried Matthew's hat on and liked it a lot. "It's really cool, Matt!" he said.

When we got home, Matthew got another pat on his forehead from Thomas and a "Great job!" It was a victorious day for Matthew.

As parents, we have to strike the balance between freedom and constructive boundaries. The beauty of working through the system in this book is that it lets your child create a budget that gives them spending money. If they lose that hard-earned cash by making choices they later regret, they lose *safely*—only a small percentage of their income. What a life lesson! Living within your budget means you won't break the bank when you take a risk.

Allowing your child to control spending within their budget reminds me of the "teach a man to fish" idea. Yes, from time to time, they will buy silly things and waste their money—and probably end up regretting it. But they will also learn to value their time and work, and to weigh that against the thrill of spontaneously spending their money. That's how they learn to fish in the deep ocean waters of their lives. Though the ocean of the personal finance world is often beautiful and calm, it can also be unpredictable. Anything can happen to anyone, even to our children, good or bad.

When our children grow older, they will fall from their safe nests and suffer, just like eaglets. They will face financial challenges in their lives—paying off heavy school loans, making payments on their credit cards, losing jobs, facing foreclosures or bankruptcies, going through business failures, making wrong investment choices, and so on.

We parents often say to our children, "I will never let anything bad happen to you, I promise." But is that really true? We are just like Marlin, the over-protective clownfish dad in the movie *Finding Nemo*. In this movie, Marlin's son, Nemo, is unexpectedly captured from his ocean home and taken to Sydney. In the course of Marlin's desperate search for Nemo, he meets Dory, to whom he says, "I promised I'd never let anything happen to him."

"Well, you can't *never* let anything happen to him," Dory replies. "Then *nothing* would ever happen to him. Not much fun for little Harpo."[2] And Marlin discovers that she is right.

We have to embrace the fact that we can't *never* let anything happen to our children, especially in the area of personal finance. On the contrary—things will always happen in our children's lives, whether we like it or not. They will experience many setbacks and crises. It's just a part of life, a growing process. Setbacks are setups for comebacks, and every crisis presents both danger and opportunity. Life will always happen, and our children will occasionally fall. The

---

2 http://www.imdb.com/title/tt0266543/quotes

important thing is how quickly they can get back up and resume moving forward.

Some parents are quick to bail out their young children (or even their older ones) every time they face difficulties in life. The consequence is that those children never learn to fly on their own, and they make the same mistakes over and over again.

"Don't quit. Suffer now and live the rest of your life as a champion,"[3] said Muhammad Ali, the legendary American boxer. Ali demonstrated throughout his life what it meant to suffer for a greater success.

When we think of success, freedom, and independence, we often think of the American bald eagle. Its long life, great strength, and majestic appearance made the eagle the US national emblem. American bald eagles are not concerned about threats from other birds because of their size, power, and their ferocity. This seemingly larger-than-life bird can easily identify their prey with their great vision and catch it with ease. Eagles are known to use the wind of the storm to rise higher instead of fleeing from it like other birds.

Do you want your children to soar like eagles or scratch like chickens? If dangerous animals attack them, who will survive?

---

3 http://www.brainyquote.com/search_results.html?q=Don%E2%80%99t+quit.+Suffer+now+and+live+the+rest+of+your+life+as+a+champion%2C%E2%80%9D+

I believe that if we teach our children at a young age to take charge of their finances and their lives—just as a mother eagle trains her eaglets to fly on their own—our children will soar. Eagles fly high, and so can our children.

Our trip to the Farmer's Market was a first for more than one reason. Yes, it was a first for Jason and Matthew to take control of spending their money for themselves, calculate tax, and tuck away their receipts. But more than anything else, it was the first time they seriously thought about the value of money and conquered the temptation to buy things on impulse.

For many of us, frivolously spending *a little* money is a way to feel peaceful and to reward ourselves. This is also the subtle message our children learn when they control their own spending. They gain the confidence to reward themselves in a reasonable way. They learn a lesson about thinking for themselves.

Yes, our children copy our words, deeds, and attitudes. They mimic our generosity, our fear, and our expectations. But just watching can't teach them the deep pleasure of giving something you worked hard for to another person. Learning the joy of sharing gives our children the most human of rewards. Our Farmer's Market trip didn't end with the boys walking away with just stuff for themselves—they walked away with the joy of having given to someone else. We'll talk about that in the next chapter.

THE TAKEAWAY

Give your child a safe place to test their money skills in the real world. Let them make decisions about spending their own money, even if they buy something they later regret.

Chapter Seven

Habit #7:
Give Back and
Share the Love

Remember the day when I took Jason and Matthew to the LA Farmer's Market for their first "eagle flight" training? You know how the story went, right? They got super excited at first, and then ended up not buying anything fancy, just a couple of small items. They had lots of money still sitting in their wallets at the end of the day.

So what happened afterward? This is a very interesting part of the story.

Jason gently stopped his brother shortly after we walked out of the toy store. They both felt sad and slightly disappointed.

"Matt, how much do you have?" he asked, looking inside his own wallet. "Let's buy Mommy a cup of coffee!"

When they began talking about that, I walked ahead of them, passing one of my favorite coffee stores. On restful weekends, this was a frequent destination after getting fresh fruits and veggies for breakfast or after eating a big, delicious Brazilian BBQ at the market.

"Okay!" I heard Matthew say. He ran up to me. "Mommy, do you want hazelnut?" In the air was the aroma of freshly ground, toasted hazelnut from the store nearby.

"Of course," I said as he and I strolled along, holding hands. "You know what I like."

So off we went to the coffee store. They ordered my hazelnut coffee, paid for it, and added some milk and sugar. They were all smiles as they handed me the hot, sweet, toasty coffee.

I was deeply touched, and felt that they'd just emerged as new butterflies from their cocoon of money management. And that day, I joyfully sipped my hazelnut coffee for a very long time.

Stepping into the Joy of Sharing

Their Morning Stuff Allowance has continued ever since they were six years old. Even after almost five years, their routines haven't changed much. They get up at 6:00 a.m. and spend the rest of the morning productively. They do all the Morning Stuff by themselves, without me even saying *ppali hae* (which means "hurry up.") By 7:15, they're ready to go off to school.

But what has changed is how they view their money since they've begun earning it. Now they have real money in their piggy banks and wallets, in their local bank, and in their investment accounts. Instead of becoming greedy for *more, more, more,* they began to think of other people. They began to appreciate their mommy and daddy for their love and care, and they wanted to use their money to buy things for their parents.

"Giving is true having,"[1] Charles Spurgeon famously said. The job of teaching my boys about earning, saving, and using money wouldn't be complete without also teaching them that having enough means giving to others. The first year in which we began the Morning Stuff Allowance and Special Incentive Project, they used their money to buy a birthday gift for each of their aunties, Amy and Nancy.

One day, Matthew bought a small vending machine toy— Winnie the Pooh—for Auntie Amy's birthday gift and gave it to her at her birthday dinner. The big smile on her face was all the reward he needed. Afterward, he told me that her smile

---

1   http://www.brainyquote.com/quotes/keywords/giving_13.html

made him happy. Later that year, at Auntie Nancy's birthday celebration, the boys joyously gave her a gift from the local discount store and received the same enthusiastic smiles and thanks from her.

To their Aunties, it didn't matter that these gifts were small and inexpensive—these were the best gifts in the whole world because they had been purchased with Jason's and Matthew's hard-earned money. They were proud of their generous nephews.

As the boys learned how to spend money within their budgets, they also learned the art and joy of giving. They loved the delight the recipients took in their gifts, and this encouraged them to keep sharing even more.

Mom's Birthday Wish List

"Mom, are you done with your birthday wish list?"

In our home, we have a tradition: we write a wish list and put it on the refrigerator for special events like our birthdays or Christmases. Interestingly, a few years ago, Jason and Matthew made some sort of agreement between them that Jason would buy things for Daddy and Matthew would buy for Mommy. They've been pretty consistent so far, and it works perfectly for all of us.

Early one Saturday morning in February, Matthew popped this question yet again when he and I were riding our scooters, exploring our new neighborhood. "Do you know what you want this year, Mom?" he asked.

I wasn't really thinking about my birthday gifts; I was just enjoying sharing time with Matthew. My boys and I liked going on scooter adventures, and we rode to many different places—some of them hours away.

"Not yet," I replied, out of breath and gasping for air. We were riding uphill, and even athletic Matthew was sweating and breathing hard. "But I will soon! Let's go home." We were both tired and it was getting hot, so home we went.

My birthday is in May and it was still far away, but Matthew had already asked that question quite a few times because, I guess, he wanted to prepare in advance. Ever since he began saving the allowance he earned by doing various jobs, Matthew has always bought something for me on special occasions.

May is the busiest month of the year for the three boys in my family because it contains Mother's Day, our wedding anniversary, and my birthday. And everyone in the family knows that each of those days has to be celebrated in its own unique way, because I like a good surprise!

Several years ago, eight-year-old Matthew had saved a little more than $100. He said, "Mommy, I can buy you anything you want up to $100 this year for your Christmas gift. So think of something really nice. Don't worry about money, okay?"

How many moms in the world get to hear something like this from an elementary-school-age son? I did!

That year, he bought me two blouses and a pair of fine blue earrings at one of my favorite retail stores. Since he had some money left over, he decided to treat me and his cousin from Korea, Sejin, to something special. We went to the Farmer's Market, where he bought us coffee and delicious coffee cake. The following year, he bought me my beloved red scooter, Reddy. "Mommy liked to ride our small scooter before, but she tripped and fell a lot," Matthew explained to his daddy. "It hurt her back so much that I wanted to buy her an adult scooter so that she can ride comfortably. That's how I found Reddy."

So what did I want for my birthday this year? It took a while to finish my 2015 Birthday Wish List. Finally I came up with the three items and put the list on the refrigerator: I wanted a journal, a digital photo frame, and a harmonica.

"This is great, Mom!" Matthew shouted when he saw the list on the refrigerator. "After I am done with my homework, we'll go to the store together and see which one you like the most. Oh! We can also check online and compare the prices!"

"Great!" I said. That night, as promised, he came back to my room after he was done with his homework and we checked out different digital photo frames and harmonicas online. He said that he would be able to save enough money before my birthday, and that he would buy me two of my favorite items. And he did! He bought me a digital photo frame and a harmonica!

"The future belongs to those who believe in the beauty of their dreams," Eleanor Roosevelt once said. I want to add, "And also to those who believe in the beauty of sharing."

My boys learned how to share their own fortune with others, starting with each other, then learning to share with their parents and other family members, and eventually sharing with their friends at school and their community at large. That's the true beauty of sharing, I believe.

We are members of a local church where Thomas and I tithe a portion of our income, and we taught them to do the same when they were a little older. When they were too young to understand the importance of tithing, they often asked why we gave our money away when we let Jason and Matthew put the money in the tithing plate as it was passed around. So we explained that it was to help the church do its good works.

And as they grew and we progressed in their financial education, it was important to me that they understand the deeper meaning of the privilege of being able to give to others. They'd seen the regular giving at church, they'd seen their father's generosity to a young pregnant girl begging for money, and they'd seen that we enjoyed making others happy.

125

Once I asked the boys—who were in second or third grade at that time—what they would do if they had a million dollars. Jason answered, "I would give a lot of money to churches so that they would be encouraged to preach the word of God to more people."

Matthew said, "I would give a pretty big portion of money to charities that go to third-world countries. I want the children in those countries to have food to eat and toys to play with."

My prayer is that these generous boys will continue to grow to be the men they were created to be, and to make a difference in other people's lives by sharing their wealth.

Their Fourth-Grade Field Trip

By the time they were nine years old, the boys were working harder and earning more money. They also had gained more financial intelligence, which enabled them to think creatively.

Ever since kindergarten, Jason and Matthew have enjoyed going on school field trips with the other kids in their class. School field trips give them opportunities to open their eyes and experience the bigger world outside the school fence, and to have good times with their friends.

Their fourth-grade class was scheduled to go on a field trip to the Irvine Park Railroad in Orange County, California. The trip would cost each student twenty dollars. When the field trip day was around the corner, their teacher told her students that thirty out of thirty-four students would need to have money for the field trip, but only about twenty-eight had paid for it at that time. The class didn't have enough money to go.

Some of the students just couldn't afford the fee and would have to stay behind. Jason and Matthew were sad that the whole class wouldn't go together and that there was a chance the entire field trip could be cancelled due to the lack of funds.

"Some of our classmates are poor and can't pay the money, but every kid wants to go," they told Thomas and me over dinner that night. "We want to help the class." Following that conversation, they brainstormed with their friend, Wesley, and came up with the idea of creating the Field Trip Fund.

When I began writing this chapter, I asked them to remember the Field Trip Fund and their first fundraising experience. Here's what they said:

One afternoon, they met with Wesley to go around the neighborhood asking people to donate money for a good cause.

"It was a regular day, so we thought that people would be home by that time," Jason and Matthew explained together, beaming with excitement. "Our goal was to raise seventy dollars, so we went to Wesley's grandmother's house first, because we know how nice she is." Wesley's grandmother was very kind to my boys and often gave them ice cream and snacks when they went over there to play with Wesley. "She gave us twenty dollars right off the bat!"

That was an encouraging start, and it helped them keep the momentum going during the rest of the afternoon. They rode their scooters around the neighborhood to find people who would donate to their cause. There were a few rejections here and there, but they didn't mind. They ended up knocking on the door of a very nice couple who wanted to help them.

"They wanted to see the proof that this fundraising was indeed for a school project, not just kids wanting money to buy alcohol or do bad stuff," Matthew said. Then they both laughed at the part where they had to ride their scooters all the way back to Wesley's grandmother's house just to get the Field Trip form they'd accidentally left there.

"We were tired and it was quite a distance. But we rode all the way back to her house and came back to get money from them." They sighed, remembering how long an afternoon it had been.

Once this couple was able to verify that these three elementary-school boys were doing what they said they were doing, those generous people gave them forty dollars. Their hard work was richly rewarded! After that, someone else also gave them another ten dollars. By now, it was getting dark, so they called it a day with a total of seventy dollars for the field trip. They had made their goal! To support their efforts, Thomas and I also gave them twenty dollars.

They brought the whole amount to their teacher the next day. Their surprised teacher used the unexpected funds to cover some of the students' field trip fees and administrative costs, and she gave thirty-two dollars back to the boys.

To make ending to this story even better, those three boys donated that money to "Jump Rope for Heart[2]," a fundraising event sponsored by the American Heart Association and the American Alliance for Health, Physical Education, Recreation, and Dance (AAHPERD).

They could have used the leftover money for themselves, but they didn't. Why? "Instead of wasting money on ourselves, we wanted to use the money to help others who need the money more than we do," explained Jason.

Their efforts weren't part of a superhero scene in which a big and powerful action hero saves the world from a catastrophic event. It's more like a starfish story, in which a young man picks up stranded starfish on the sand, one by one, and gently tosses each one back into the water.

In this Field Trip Fund story, three fourth-grade students made a subtle yet lifelong difference in the lives of some of

---

2 http://www.heart.org/HEARTORG/Giving/ForIndividuals/Joinan
Event/Jump-Rope-for-Heart-Event_UCM_315609_SubHomePage.jsp

their classmates. And as with most good deeds, we'll never fully know what that meant to the kids who otherwise wouldn't have been able to go.

I tell this story because it illustrates so much. First, it shows that my boys had learned by example that we can all help each other. They saw it in church, at the store, in the bank manager's generosity to them, and in their teacher's patience and kindness with her students. Second, they knew that when we have enough, we give to those who don't. Third, they learned that they can reach a higher goal with teamwork.

Good collaboration is a way to blend minds, bodies, and hearts. Without the heart part, collaboration tends to produce rote, scripted results. With heart, collaboration gives creativity free rein. But to give our hearts to someone else, we should FLY—First Love Yourself. If we don't love ourselves, it's impossible to love others. But when we first love ourselves, we can love others and it can make everything perfect—as Jason once told me in a very poetic way.

"Mommy," Jason asked out of the blue, "do you know what makes everything perfect?" We were getting ready to go to the park to play. He was four years old at that time.

"What is it?" I asked, a little puzzled.

"It's love, Mommy. When you love me, I am perfect. When I love you, you are perfect. Love is what makes everything perfect."

I stared into his innocent, dark brown eyes in amazement. "You are right, Jason," I said, patting him on his forehead with tears in my eyes.

Love is the answer for all, and that's all we need. As the missionary Amy Carmichael famously said, "You can give without loving, but you cannot love without giving." Where there is love, there is life through giving and sharing, and that's how love lasts forever.

"Let us not be satisfied with just giving money. Money is not enough, money can be got, but they need your hearts to love them. So, spread your love everywhere you go."
—*Mother Teresa*

"You have to find what sparks a light in you, so that you, in your own way, can illuminate the world."
—*Oprah Winfrey*

The day my boys bought me the first coffee cup at the LA farmer's market with their allowance

Sunny and Reddy!   *My excellent boys!*

THE TAKEAWAY

Learning to be generous with others is a gift to ourselves. Help your children notice the many little ways they can give to someone else through small gifts or generous actions.

Conclusion

Teaching our children about anything is a form of love. Teaching them about finances is a loving investment in their future. And that's what this book has been about.

By working to establish the habits in this book, you have just put your child ahead of the curve. Once they're teenagers, they can take the next step toward more sophisticated, complex money management. You can use the websites listed in Habit 5, and you can visit my website (www.nomoneymonster.com), where you can download valuable money-management tools for your kids. You'll also find advice on meeting your growing child's more mature and complex financial needs.

My hope is for all children to have the advantage of being Money Masters of their lives, rather than Money Monsters in their families and in society.

We began this book talking about how children who don't learn money skills can drown in financial privation and struggle all their lives just to survive. Even children who are born into affluence may be unfortunate enough to have parents who use monetary indulgence as a substitute for investing their personal time. Either way, these children can grow up to become Money Monsters who suffer from poverty or who spend wildly, indulging every self-destructive whim. Money Masters are those who have learned the skills your child stands to learn from this book, and who can use them to build a life of security and happiness. Here is a quick recap of the habits your children should have learned, or are working on developing now:

- They understand that a healthy mindset about money produces a healthy financial future. (Habit 1)
- They know that their personal money is a result of their personal efforts. (Habit 1)
- They save their money, putting it first into a piggy bank, and then into an interest bearing bank account and then into an investment account for higher growth potential. (Habit 2)
- They learn how to perform basic banking tasks, and they feel like a million bucks at their own bank. (Habit 2)
- They reward themselves by taking a small portion of their earnings to use for fun or for things they desire. (Habit 3)
- They take care of themselves in the morning with a good attitude to get the sure rewards. (Habit 3)

- They learn time management and self-discipline as well as good reading and writing skills. (Habit 3)
- They understand that the way to achieve success is through setting high goals and then accomplishing them. (Habit 4)
- They learn to stay disciplined and track their progress for more rewards and recognitions. (Habit 4)
- They understand what the US monetary system is about, so they can use it to their advantage and to help others. (Habit 5)
- They know which Internet resources have the info they need to learn more about personal finance. (Habit 5)
- They understand that hidden costs are a part of life. They know how to look for such costs and can add it to the price of a purchase. (Habit 6)
- They know that it feels good to help others. (Habit 7)
- They understand that money is essential to life, but isn't the *reason* for life. Life is for living, loving and sharing well. (Habit 7)

Children who learn money skills early are more successful. If we spread the word and teach these skills, there will be less poverty and more blessings. Let's put our young children on the path toward financial literacy, security and independence. Let's raise a world of educated, confident children who make smart financial choices—a world of Money Masters!

About the Author

Author Sunny Lee is a respected and trusted financial advisor serving clients from all walks of life in Southern California. She is the owner and CEO of Good Life Advisors, a full service insurance and IAR® (Investment Advisor Representative) company in Torrance, California. As a bi-lingual advisor, she can guide your financial needs in English or Korean.

She has reached MDRT (Million Dollar Round Table) for six consecutive years, and also an author of the Korean personal finance book *Mr. & Mrs. Millionaire* and currently resides in Rancho Palos Verdes, California, with her husband Thomas and her twin boys Jason and Matthew.

Find her at www.nomoneymonster.com or contact her: sunnylee@goodlifeinc.net

100 Inspiring Quotes

Quote for the Day	Date/ Sign	Date/ Sign	Date/ Sign	Date/ Sign
Always do your best. What you plant now, you will harvest later.				
Dream no small dreams for they have no power to move the hearts of men.				
Be the change that you wish to see in the world.				
Expect problems and eat them for breakfast.				
Start by doing what's necessary, then do what is possible, and suddenly you are doing the impossible.				
Weekly Review & Credit:				
Success is a progressive realization of worthy ideal.				
Whatever the mind can conceive and believe, it can achieve.				
Future belongs to those who believe in the beauty of their dreams.				
Failure is an event, not a person. Yesterday ended last night.				
You become what you think about. (10)				
Weekly Review & Credit:				

Necessity is the mother of invention.				
Don't judge by the harvest you reap but by the seeds that you plant.				
The man who has no imagination has no wings.				
Imagination is your preview of life's coming attractions.				
Logic will get you from A to B. Imagination will take you everywhere.				
Weekly Review & Credit:				
Reality is for those who lack imagination.				
Don't go through life. Grow through life.				
You will never be brave if you don't get hurt.				
You reap what you sow.				
Sometimes you win, sometimes you learn.(20)				
Weekly Review & Credit:				

Quote for the Day	Date/ Sign	Date/ Sign	Date/ Sign	Date/ Sign
Asking is the beginning of receiving. Receiving is like an ocean. Don't go there with a spoon.				
Perception is awareness shaped by belief.				
Ideas are worthless unless we act on it.				
If you do what is easy, your life will be hard. If you do what is hard, your life will be easy.				
Action is character.				
Weekly Review & Credit:				
Still waters run deep.				
You can't see the picture if you are in the frame.				
Never give up. There is no such thing as an ending. Just a new beginning.				
Pain is weakness leaving the body.				
Don't quit. Suffer now and live the rest of your life as a champion. (30)				
Weekly Review & Credit:				

The only difference between a good day and a bad day is your attitude.				
Just because you have a bad day doesn't mean that you have a bad life.				
Be selective in your battles. Sometimes peace is better than being right.				
Act as though it is impossible to fail.				
You can't start the next chapter of your life if you keep re-reading the last one.				
Weekly Review & Credit:				
Life is like photography we develop from the negatives.				
You are confined only by the walls you build yourself.				
Everything you want is on the other side of fear				
Success is the ability to go from one failure to another with no loss of enthusiasm.				
Every champion was once a contender that refused to give up.(40)				
Weekly Review & Credit:				

Quote for the Day	Date/ Sign	Date/ Sign	Date/ Sign	Date/ Sign
Darkness cannot drive out darkness: only light can do that. Hate cannot drive out hate: only love can do that.				
We got what it takes, but it will take everything we've got.				
If opportunity doesn't knock, build a door.				
Do not pray for an easy life. Pray for the strength to endure a difficult one.				
The only thing worse than being blind is having sight and no vision.				
Weekly Review & Credit:				
If you want to soar in life, you must first learn to fly, first love yourself.				
Great men are not born great. They grow great.				
Kindness is a language that the deaf can hear and the blind can see.				
We can complain because rose bushes have thorns, or rejoice because thorn bushes have roses.				
I don't know what my future holds, but I do know who holds my future.(50)				
Weekly Review & Credit:				

Why fit in when you were born to standout?				
Holding on to anger is like drinking poison and expecting the other person to die.				
A friend is someone who knows all about you and still loves you.				
In order to be irreplaceable, one must always be different.				
It isn't the mountains ahead to climb that wear you down. It's the pebble in your shoe.				
Weekly Review & Credit:				

Quote for the Day	Date/ Sign	Date/ Sign	Date/ Sign	Date/ Sign
You can't stop the waves, but you can learn to surf.				
Great mind discuss ideas; average minds discuss events; small minds discuss people.				
As a man thinks in his heart, so is he.				
Stress is caused by being 'here' but wanting to be 'there.'				
He who is not courageous enough to take risks will accomplish nothing in life.(60)				
Weekly Review & Credit:				
Ask and it will be given to you; Seek and you will find; Knock and the door will be opened to you.				
I dream my painting, and then I paint my dream.				
You've gotta dance like there's nobody watching, Love like you'll never be hurt, Sing like there's nobody listening, And live like it's heaven on earth.				
Be yourself; everybody else is already taken.				
No one can make you feel inferior without your consent.				
Weekly Review & Credit:				

Always end the day with a positive thought.				
Even the darkest night will end and the sun will rise.				
No matter how hard the things were, tomorrow is a fresh opportunity to make it better.				
We don't see things as they are, we see them as we are.				
The only place where your dream becomes impossible is in your own thinking.(70)				
Weekly Review & Credit:				

Quote for the Day	Date/ Sign	Date/ Sign	Date/ Sign	Date/ Sign
Our greatest weakness lies in giving up.				
The most certain way to succeed is always to try just one more time.				
I've had a lot of worries in my life, most of which never happened.				
The past has no power over the present moment.				
No matter what the situation, remind yourself "I have a choice."				
Weekly Review & Credit:				
If we're growing, we're always going to be out of our comfort zone.				
The difference between stumbling blocks and stepping stones is how you use them.				
All things are difficult before they are easy.				
Success is falling nine times and getting up ten.				
Happiness, like unhappiness, is a proactive choice.(80)				
Weekly Review & Credit:				

Remember no pressure, no diamonds. Pressure is a part of success.				
When the world pushes you to your knees, you're in the perfect position to pray.				
When we are no longer able to change a situation, we are challenged to change ourselves.				
The best way to gain self-confidence is to do what you are afraid to do.				
You cannot tailor-make the situations in life but you can tailor-make the attitudes to fit those situations.				
Weekly Review & Credit:				

Quote for the Day	Date/ Sign	Date/ Sign	Date/ Sign	Date/ Sign
Pain is a fact; our evaluation of it is a choice.				
The greatest discovery of all time is that a person can change his future by merely changing his attitude.				
Nothing truly stops you. Nothing truly holds you back. For your own will is always within your control.				
Welcome every morning with a smile. Look on the new day as another special gift from your Creator.				
Today will never happen again. Don't waste it with a false start or no start at all. (90)				
Weekly Review & Credit:				
Sometimes you find yourself in the middle of nowhere, and sometimes in the middle of nowhere, you find yourself.				
All things are possible to him who believes.				
If you don't believe in yourself, don't expect others to believe in you.				
Ideas are worthless unless executed. They are just a multiplier. Execution is worth millions.				

Faith is putting both legs in the water.				
Weekly Review & Credit:				
Honesty is making your words conform to reality.				
Disappointment is a gap between expectation and reality.				
You are a true gift unwrapped. Open it during your lifetime.				
As we are liberated from our own fear, our presence automatically liberates others.				
Our deepest fear is that we are powerful beyond measure.(100)				
Weekly Review & Credit:				

CPSIA information can be obtained
at www.ICGtesting.com
Printed in the USA
LVOW04s0204141116
512842LV00008B/85/P